I0804957

Historic Tales of the LLANO ESTACADO

Historic Tales *of the* LLANO ESTACADO

Edited by David J. Murrah and Paul H. Carlson

The History Press

Published by The History Press
Charleston, SC
www.historypress.com

Front cover, top: courtesy Southwest Collection, Texas Tech University; *bottom*: courtesy Ellen Carlson.
Back cover: courtesy Diane McLaurin; *inset*: courtesy Ellen Carlson.

First published 2020

Manufactured in the United States

ISBN 9781467146548

Library of Congress Control Number: 2020934343

Notice: The information in this book is true and complete to the best of our knowledge. It is offered without guarantee on the part of the authors or The History Press. The authors and The History Press disclaim all liability in connection with the use of this book.

This book is dedicated to the supportive staff of the Southwest Collection at Texas Tech University, one of the nation's premier research libraries and manuscript repositories.

Contents

Contents

Preface

The Llano Estacado is a flat, semi-arid, high plateau stretching through West Texas and eastern New Mexico and situated under a vast dome of blue sky. On its eastern edge in Texas, a long, serrated escarpment cuts the Llano sharply from the Rolling Plains. Similarly, its western escarpment in New Mexico abruptly divides it from the Pecos River Valley.

Atop this large, elevated tableland, the horizon extends south from the Canadian River Valley in the Texas Panhandle some 250 miles before melting into the state's Permian Basin country, and from east to west between its escarpments the Llano Estacado spreads some 200 miles. It is a region larger than the state of Indiana.

Most scholars suggest that the name *Llano Estacado* comes from Spanish explorers and early missionaries who, traveling from New Mexico on foot or by horseback, saw from miles distant the Llano's well-defined western escarpment as a palisade or stockade and thus "stockaded plains" or Staked Plains. There are other, less compelling interpretations, of course, including an important one in this anthology, but some represent little more than western myth. It is hard to kill a myth. Yet, no longer should anyone accept the impractical idea that Spanish trailblazers carried with them across the huge empty grassland long stakes to mark the trail. They had native guides.

Our book, *Historic Tales of the Llano Estacado*, is a collection of history-based essays on the region and its informal capital, Lubbock, the largest city on the American Great Plains. The essays cover a wide variety of topics. Sometimes, they represent a fresh look at old issues related to Lubbock and the larger Southern Plains. Other times, they embody material not found in conventional studies of the huge area. Collectively, they represent a history classroom made palatable by superb storytelling; in the end, they present a fascinating and informative but nontraditional narrative of the sometimes mystifying, but always dynamic, Llano Estacado.

Accordingly, in forty-seven eight-hundred-word essays, many with illustrations, our book seeks to examine interesting personalities, events and places of Lubbock and the Llano Estacado. Our aim is to provide an unconventional account of the region, a place that receives far less attention from scholars and an educated reading public than it deserves. Together, the essays provide a considered analysis of one of the last-settled quarters of the United States.

We enjoyed much good help in putting this anthology together. Staff members at the Southwest Collection at Texas Tech University proved extraordinary helpful in the effort. Monte Monroe, archivist of the Southwest Collection, provided major support with ideas, topics to cover and conversation. Randy Vance and Caitlin Leonard and their student assistants in the collection's reference services, checked archival records, suggested photographs, found rare documents and made research a pleasant experience.

We owe a major debt of gratitude to the authors who contributed essays to this volume. They were not only cooperative and supportive but also crucial to the book's completion in a timely fashion. In sometimes different form, many of the essays appeared in the *Lubbock Avalanche-Journal* between 2016 and 2018, and we are grateful to its former associate editor, Karen Boehm, for her help.

We are likewise grateful to our wives, Ann Murrah and Ellen Carlson, for the considerable support and self-sacrifice they provided as we researched, wrote and edited the essays here. As always in the past, our wives proved invaluable in completing the book in a timely fashion.

—David J. Murrah
Rockport, Texas

—Paul H. Carlson
Ransom Canyon, Texas
January 2020

Introduction

Modern first-time travelers making their way toward New Mexico or Colorado via U.S. Highway 84 through Lubbock probably pay little attention to the rolling countryside—until they ascend to the top of what West Texans call the Caprock, just to the west of Post. There, they are stricken by the vast flatness that surrounds them. They may even echo the sentiment of one of the region's pioneer women when, seeing the plains for the first time, exclaimed, "Good Heavens! An ocean of land!"

For the most part, the so-called Caprock is what both preserves and defines the Llano Estacado. Laid down as a part of an alluvial floodplain as the once towering mountains of New Mexico eroded, the upper layer of silt eventually became a hardened, rock-like caliche. This layer provided protection from wind and water erosion and allowed the development of a layer of topsoil that in turn produced the immense grasslands and, in modern times, rich farmland.

Prominently visible along the edge of the escarpment surrounding the Llano Estacado, especially on the west and eastern slopes, the Caprock became the visible reminder of what made the High Plains. The formation marks a distinctive boundary between the High Plains and the valleys below. Its highest point lies along the Llano's northwestern escarpment in northern Curry County, New Mexico, at more than 4,900 feet.

Sloping gently downward to the east, the Llano Estacado is roughly bordered by Interstate 40 on the north and I-20 on the south. Specifically, its northern boundary is the Canadian River escarpment, running east from San Jon, New Mexico, approximately 175 miles to a point about 30 miles northeast of Pampa, Texas. Its western border follows the Pecos River escarpment southward for 300 miles, encompassing the eastern counties of southwestern New Mexico to a point about 50 miles south of Midland. The southern boundary is ill-defined and fades into the Edwards Plateau.

From its southeastern point near Midkiff, the Llano's eastern edge extends to the north approximately 350 miles toward Pampa; much of the eastern escarpment was created by the erosion of the rivers and streams that once helped to create the great floodplain. These include the Concho, Colorado, Brazos and Red rivers. The latter three once had headwaters in the New Mexico mountains until the Pecos River gradually snaked northward and literally stole their headwaters. With the loss of their water source, the once deep river canyons were gradually filled in by wind erosion, especially on the western side of the Llano. Today, the shallow depressions of Monument, Sulphur Springs, Yellow House, Running Water and Black Water draws are the only reminders of what were once major flowing streams.

The modern Llano Estacado encompasses more than 32,000 square miles, a region larger than all of New England. It is the largest non-mountainous land formation in North America. It is home to more than 1.2 million people and includes four major cities: Amarillo, Lubbock, Midland and Odessa.

The Llano Estacado has always impressed visitors as a big, broad country. As early as 1541, Francisco Vásquez de Coronado, the great explorer of New Mexico, talked about the Llano Estacado as "so vast I did not see [its] limits anywhere that I went." In those early times, the Llano appeared horizontal, uniform and ruler straight. Coronado wrote to his king, Philip V, "I reached some plains, with no more landmarks than as if we had been swallowed up the by the sea, where…there was not a stone, nor a bit of rising ground, nor a tree, nor a shrub, nor anything to go by."

More recently, the Flatlanders musician Butch Hancock playfully said, "In Lubbock you can see fifty miles in any direction. And if you stand on a tuna fish can, you can see a hundred miles." Such remarks about its celebrated topography aside, the Llano's geology and its geoarchaeology date to twelve thousand or more years ago—much longer if one digs deep below its modern surface and into its limitless pre-Holocene past of dinosaurs and briny seas.

Nonetheless, the Llano's history is mainly young and recent, but there is mystery in its past. Indeed, even the origin of its name represents a puzzle like the Gordian knot. In translation from its Spanish cognomen, the place is "Staked Plains," but for reasons hard to fathom, there is little agreement on what "Staked Plains" actually meant. Likewise, there is the myth of the

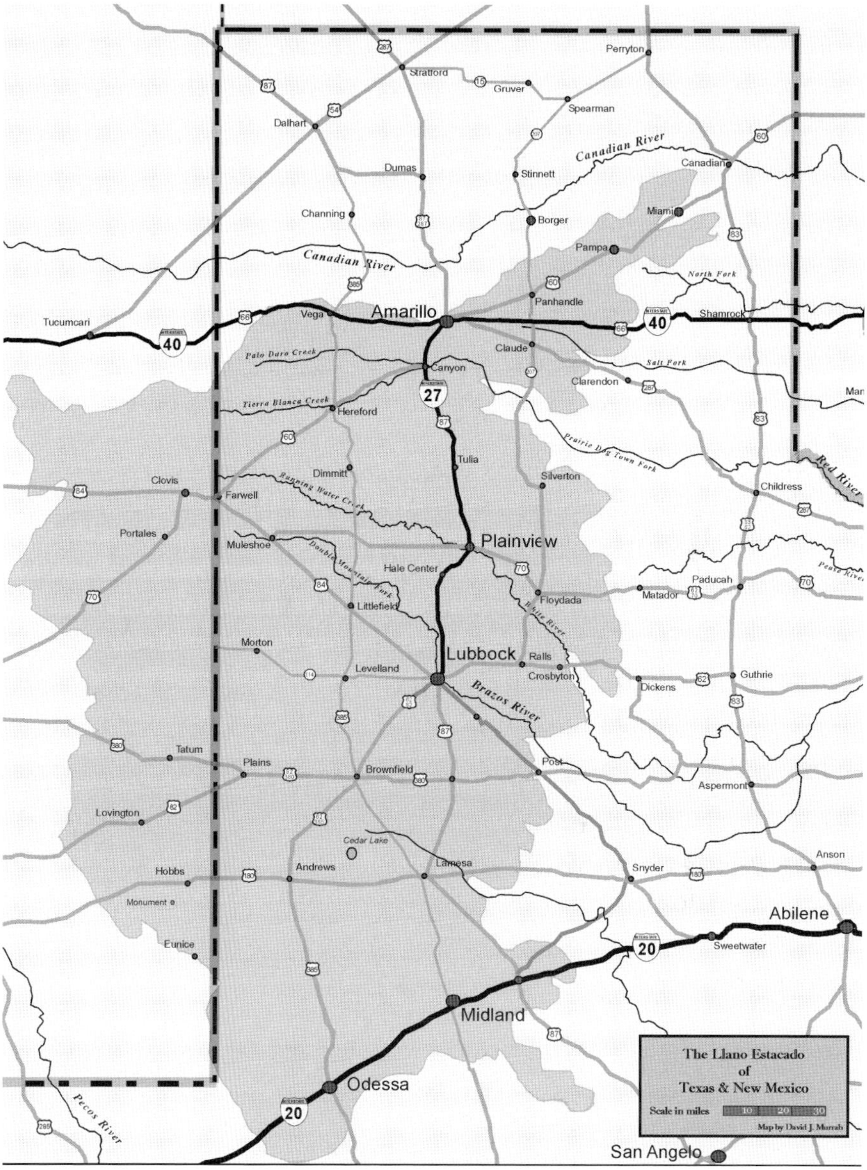

Map of The Llano Estacado of Texas and New Mexico. *Courtesy David Murrah.*

Llano Estacado as desert. Perhaps for good reason the myth persisted for nearly four hundred years. Even today, for example, to see the Llano as a desert one needs only to look at the region's low average annual rainfall; its ceaseless winds often filled with dust and grit; its dry, windy sand storms; and, as Ogallala Aquifer water levels recede, its ever-increasing return to dryland farming.

In its long premodern farming past, moreover, the Llano Estacado from midsummer to early fall in droughty years looked and felt like a desert. In hot, dry weather its playa lakes dried up; its streams ran intermittently; its sand-hill grasses thinned; and particularly its buffalo and grama grasses turned brown and curled in on themselves, giving off the appearance of an utterly flat, sunburnt and arid wasteland.

And, in fact, plenty of early reports speak of the desert-like plains. Pedro Castañeda, official chronicler of the Francisco Coronado expedition, wrote about going "without water for many days." Coronado, himself, in the October 1541 letter to his king, wrote that they traveled "across these deserts for seventy-five days." But the thirty-one-year-old Spanish commander also wrote positively about the Llano: there "is much fine pasture land, with good grass." Notwithstanding Coronado's favorable remark about good pasture, the desert myth persisted. Government explorers, such as Randolph B. Marcy, who crossed it in 1849, 1852 and 1855, called the Llano Estacado such names as the "great Sahara of North America."

There was something mysterious about the Llano Estacado. Cattle drovers avoided it. Stagecoach and mail routes went around it. American soldiers got lost on it, and for years it remained the private preserve of Comanches and their moveable bison commissary. Finally, in 1875, William Shafter began changing the perception. Shafter led a military expedition across the Llano Estacado and, despite at times suffering desperately for lack of water, wrote favorably on the region. In his lengthy official report, he noted several times the existence of "good grass," reliable water and existing wagon roads.

Although the desert myth persisted for a time, soon after Shafter's expedition, sheepherders, such as Casimero Romero, and cattlemen, such as Charles Goodnight and C.C. Slaughter, pushed their flocks and herds onto the Llano Estacado. Farmer-stockmen, such as Henry Clay Smith, settled into the Llano's canyon lands, and pioneers, such as the Quaker farmers and townspeople with Paris Cox at Estacado, came close behind.

People organized town and county governments and built homes, businesses, schools and churches. Railroads arrived. Farming, especially cotton production, replaced cattle ranching on the Llano, and the region grew in population—although it has never been large.

Unfortunately, when railroads bypassed communities or when they lost a county seat vote, towns disappeared. Many schools in the wake of major consolidation in the 1930s and again in the 1950s disappeared or, because of declining student populations in rural areas, closed.

Natural disasters also impacted the region. Dust storms, tornados, occasional bitter cold winters, hail, prolonged drought and random floods created dangerous hazards for humans and animals alike.

In the heart of this great circle of unpredictable weather, horizontal topography and big blue sky sits Lubbock, the largest city on the Llano Estacado—"sand-scrubbed," as a former resident described it, but in 2020 growing with remarkable energy and vitality.

Founded in 1890, Lubbock is a young city, but the story of its brief past stands near the center of the mystery, myth and lore of the "stockaded plains." Its history in concert with tales of the larger Llano Estacado as portrayed in these lively essays form the "Tales" of this book.

Part I

A UNIQUE COUNTRY

The Llano Estacado is indeed a unique land, a place that took thousands of years to create to its present form of windswept plains. Its present topography reflects its formative heritage, with ranges of sand dunes, ancient forests of dwarfed shinnery oak and playa lakes and springs that have provided precious water for its inhabitants.

As you will see in this part, rainfall and drought—still the watchwords of its present occupants—have been the major factors in not only shaping the Llano, but also in determining the nature and quantity of its inhabitants.

Over the centuries, as the region became drier, its scattered springs and lakes helped to concentrate wildlife, thereby providing food for the earliest of human cultures—Clovis and Folsom peoples. Thousands of years later, a few lakes remained to save the lives of the 1877 Buffalo Soldier expedition.

1

Late Pleistocene Extinctions

Paul H. Carlson

At one time, the Llano Estacado hosted some of the most exotic animals in the world. These included ancient horses, large bison, dog-sized camels, four-horn antelope, woolly and Columbian mammoths, mastodons, giant armadillos, ground sloths nearly as big as elephants, giant anteaters, dire wolves, tapirs, short-faced bears and many large rodents.

But they all disappeared in the late Pleistocene era that began about 15,000 years ago. Mass extinctions of animal, plant and aquatic life have occurred on Earth more than a dozen times since life began some 4 billion years ago. The worst such extinction event appeared 250 million years ago at the boundary between the Permian and Triassic periods, when 95 percent of all land animals died—and seemingly all at once.

The most famous mass extinction occurred about 65 or 66 million years ago at the Cretaceous-Tertiary (K-T) boundary, when a giant meteor or comet struck the planet, triggering a catastrophic crisis that ended the age of dinosaurs. The Pleistocene (or Ice Age) extinctions began between 15,000 to 10,000 years ago during the last years of the late Pleistocene epoch. Large numbers of animal species perished.

In Europe, during the late Pleistocene die-off, the death of species was relatively small, but elsewhere around the globe, the extinctions were massive. Perhaps 86 percent of the large animals of Australia became extinct, many of them even before 15,000 years ago.

Paul Carlson poses with this replica of a giant armadillo at the Lubbock Lake Landmark. The animal once roamed the Llano Estacado. Some were as large as a small bear. *Courtesy Monte Monroe.*

In South America, large animal species, such as tapirs and giant rodents, suffered an 80 percent loss, and in North America, including the Southern Great Plains and the Llano Estacado, the percentage of loss for large animal species may have reached beyond 66 percent.

Reasons for the great die-off at the Pleistocene-Holocene (modern epoch) boundary remain something of a puzzle. A few theories describe such influences as disease epidemics, accidental change of sex ratios, astronomical agents, the beginning of agriculture and others. Some of the most passionate, and most popular, arguments suggest overhunting by early humans, but the majority of explanations cite changing climate and weather patterns at the end of the last great Ice Age—the Wurm-Weichsel-Wisconsin glaciation.

As glaciers retreated at the end of the Ice Age, the climate and weather patterns warmed, ecosystems changed and vegetation types shifted. On the Great Plains, for example, tall, coarse grass savannahs that supported large mammals disappeared in favor of short grasses and spreading forest lands. The tundra of northern Europe, Asia and North America shrunk, also adversely affecting large mammals. Smaller mammals could adjust and move into empty ecological niches. The largest species, particularly sensitive to climatic change, had no such chance. They could move, certainly, but their grazing and foraging zones became smaller and spread apart over greater distances.

Scientists who maintain that humans played a significant role in the Pleistocene extinctions go further. Noting that extinctions at the end of Ice Ages are not evident in the plant kingdom, they suggest that overhunting by humans made a devastating impact on animal populations already in decline. Many animals had no significant defense system to use against humans, creatures with whom they had not long been in contact. Bison, particularly ancient straight-horn bison, when confronted with danger as from wolves, for example, tended to cluster, with bulls or large females on the outside facing the threat. Such a defense arrangement worked well against wolves, even large dire wolves, and saber-toothed cats. But against humans with spears, the defense pattern was nearly useless. Human overkill, as a result, became the difference between extinction and survival of animal species.

In North America, the argument goes, early hunter-gatherers came south from Alaska. They found a rich, mild environment that supported immense herds of ancient bison and large numbers of other game, such as four-horn antelope, mammoths, mastodons and ancient horses and camels no larger than llamas. Because of the abundant animal-food resources, the human population increased rapidly, and people made their way quickly through and across the steppe-like plains environment. As they moved, the argument continues, they hunted some animals—large herbivores especially—into extinction. Ancient carnivores, such as saber-toothed cats, dependent on the same big game, perished.

Whatever the causes, in North America, two-thirds of the large mammals present when humans first arrived disappeared. Extinction scholar Paul S.

Martin has noted that at least thirty-one genera of large herbivores vanished in the big die-off, thus placing pressure on carnivores, scavengers and other creatures ecologically dependent on the grass-eaters. Pronghorns, deer, elk, bighorn sheep, moose, wolves, coyotes and other species survived the onslaught, as did many smaller animals, such as foxes, jackrabbits, prairie dogs and squirrels.

Nonetheless, the die-off at the end of the Pleistocene epoch changed life on the Southern Plains. It may have contributed to the demise of Clovis people in our area about 10,800 years ago and Folsom people about 10,200 years ago. Perhaps the Pleistocene extinctions represent important reasons that humans turned to agriculture.

2

Greatest of Droughts

The Altithermal

Paul H. Carlson

Altithermal" is a geological and climatic designation for an extensive period of drought that occurred across the Great Plains beginning about 6,500 years ago (or 4,500 BCE). The Altithermal event occurred on the Llano Estacado during what many archaeologists call the "Archaic" period, about 8,500 years ago to about 2,000 years ago. For our area, many scholars subdivide the Archaic into three chronological parts, with the big drought coming in the middle of the three (6,500 years ago to about 4,500 years ago), well after glaciers at the end of the Ice Age had retreated.

Also known by experts as the Atlantic Climate Phase or the Holocene Climate Optimum, the long—two-thousand-year—intermittent dry spell brought changes to what some call the North American shortgrass steppe, including, writes Margaret Bickers, "the South Plains, the Llano Estacado, and the High Plains of eastern New Mexico and Colorado into northern Kansas." Bison and other large fauna left the region for a while, and people followed, moving east to wetter country or west to higher elevations. Many did not return to the plains, writes Bickers, "for several thousand years."

During the long drought, tall grass prairie characteristic of the region gave way to shortgrass steppe, and in the most severe instances, the short grasses tended to give way to desert shrubs and near-desert conditions. Some places became nearly bare of vegetation, and, accordingly, a few scientists argue that during the long Altithermal, a western Great Basin desert culture emerged on the Great Plains.

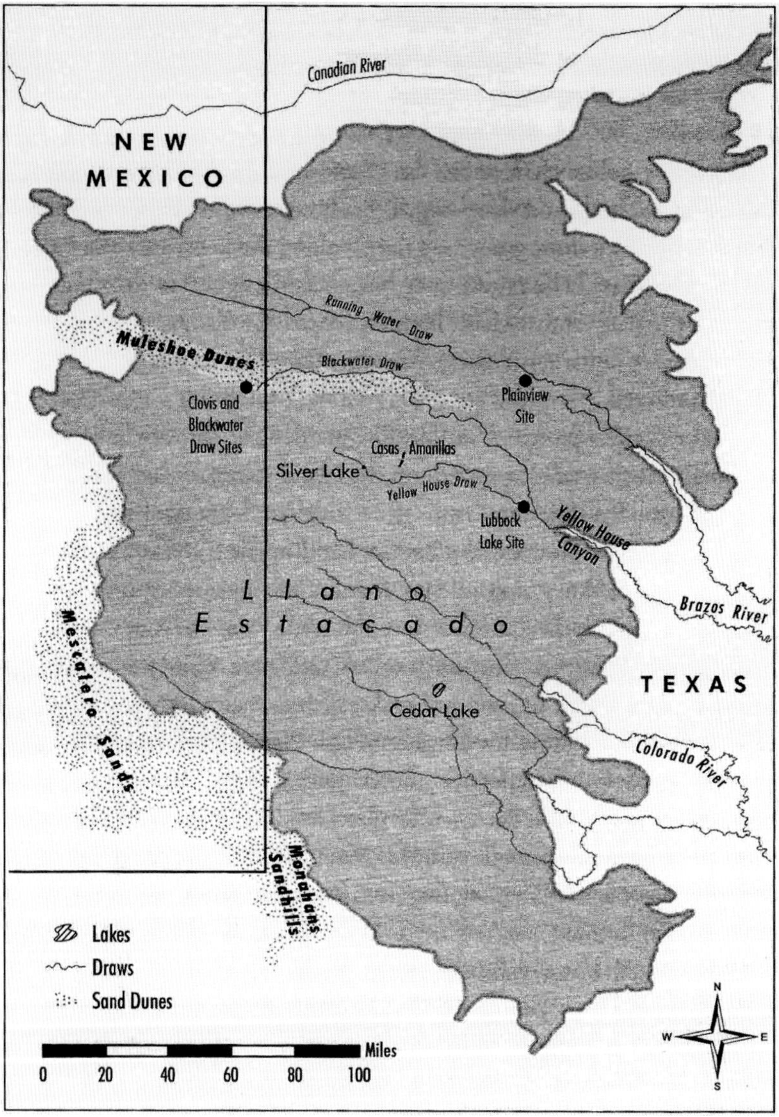

The important archaeological sites on the Llano Estacado are located along the draws that cross the region. *Courtesy Curtis Peoples.*

Not unlike drought in our area in the 1930s and 1950s, during the Altithermal, wind picked up soil from the thinning ground. This time, however, the wind through two millennia deposited the material in dunes, draws and valleys, helping to create some of the huge local dunes and choking off and filling in the upper Yellow House and Blackwater draws of the ancient Portales

River Valley. Moreover, as grasses thinned, bison and other large mammals on the plains declined in number and moved elsewhere.

Archaic-age people living in the area adapted. Many left. Others turned more and more to plant foods and hunted smaller animals, such as pronghorns and jackrabbits. Those who remained probably tended to stay near streams and rivers that held permanent water sources. The Lubbock Lake Site, for example, held water during the Altithermal, and the archaeological record suggests it supported a human population throughout the long drought.

Causes for the Altithermal are not precisely known. Increased sunspot activity is one theory. Most theories suggest changes in atmospheric air masses and wind patterns. Three air masses characterize much of the interior of North America: the Arctic, the Tropical Maritime and the Mild Pacific.

The dry Mild Pacific air mass dominates the Great Plains for about 50 percent of the year and probably accounts for the grassland environment. It occurs through much of the winter and part of the summer, times when the region receives very little rainfall.

Arctic and Tropical Maritime air masses carrying greater precipitation intrude on the Mild Pacific in late winter and early summer, bringing rain in the spring. Also, the Tropical Maritime, which brings rains to the eastern prairies, sometimes intrudes in early autumn into the Mild Pacific, bringing rain in late summer and early fall.

Seasonal changes in the three air masses, governed in part by the waxing and waning of the upper tropic and subtropic jet streams, impact rainfall amounts. A year-round dominance of the Mild Pacific results in severe drought.

In the case of the Altithermal, a major shift in the three air masses may have led to a centuries-long dominance of the Mild Pacific. If so, the Arctic and Tropical Maritime air masses did not bring significant rains to the Llano Estacado. Drought followed. As in modern times, however, varying degrees of severity, both geographically and climatically, characterized the Altithermal. There were years of heavier rainfall.

Yet, over time, western shortgrass plains and climate extended into eastern tallgrass prairies. Grasses thinned in our region, forage yields declined and the carrying capacity of the High Plains decreased. Large herbivores left, seeking drought refuge elsewhere.

As indicated, Archaic-age people adapted. They shot waterfowl, hunted deer and foraged for many species of wild plant foods, including prairie turnips, groundnuts, cactus fruits, sunflowers, Jerusalem artichokes and seasonal fruits. They paid close attention to changing grazing conditions and carefully monitored the movements of the smaller, curved-horn species of bison that was emerging. They developed a variety of communal hunts to secure animal food.

When in the late Archaic period, after 4,500 years ago, the climate turned wetter and probably a bit cooler, the Altithermal ended and people adapted yet again.

In summary, causes for the long drought remain speculative, but a shift in air masses, jet streams and ocean currents may have played a key role.

3

The Lakes of Lynn County

Paul H. Carlson

Over much of the Llano Estacado, there are a number of wet-weather (playa) lakes, and many are found in Lynn County. Of these, several lakes hold water through the year, and some of them have been the site of significant events in our region's past.

The lakes, all alkali, include several along U.S. Highway 87: Guthrie, Nance, Dew Drop and Skeen lakes. In addition, Double Lakes, known in the nineteenth century as Lagunas Cuates and Lagunas Quartes, is west-northwest of Tahoka, and Tahoka Lake (Laguna Tahoka in the nineteenth century), the largest of the Lynn County lakes, can be seen to the east of Texas Highway 400 between Tahoka and Wilson.

Although there are plenty of additional playas, other "lakes" include Three Lakes, located southwest of Tahoka; Frost Lake southwest of Tahoka on the Dawson County line; Gooch Lake southwest of Tahoka along Lost Draw; and Mound Lake west-northwest of Tahoka on the Terry County line.

Tahoka Lake, Double Lakes and Mound Lake usually hold water year-round. Along with Guthrie Lake, they have been the sites of notable events in Llano Estacado history. And, of course, through generations, they served as major camping grounds for Native Americans.

The first Europeans, Spaniards, in the area may have made use of Tahoka and Guthrie lakes, as in some ways they connected Punta del Agua (Lubbock Lake Site) with the upper reaches of the South Fork (main fork) of the

Tahoka Lake is one of the largest natural lakes on the Llano Estacado. *Courtesy Austin Allison.*

Double Mountain Fork of the Brazos River and Bull and Tobacco creeks, which form the upper ends of the Colorado River.

In 1875, Lieutenant Colonel William R. Shafter with his Tenth Cavalry soldiers connected by wagon roads many of the larger Llano Estacado lakes, including many of those in Lynn County. He camped for several days at Double Lakes, rode along old bison and Indian trails between Tahoka Lake and the Muchaque ("Moo-cha-ko-way," as Shafter spelled it) area around Mushaway Peak in Borden County. He also marked trails between Double Lakes and Cedar Lake (Laguna Sabinas) in present-day Gaines County and Double Lakes and Punta del Agua.

They found a few signs of Indians at Tahoka Lake: abandoned camps and some old, broken tipi polls, but little else. Nonetheless, historian Martin Crimmings said that Tahoka Lake was a favorite Comanche camping place, as there were freshwater springs available.

There is also a legend of buried treasure—Spanish gold—near Tahoka Lake, but none has been reported as found. Apparently, Spanish and Mexican miners dug for gold in the Croton Breaks near present-day Dickens and Spur and in the mountains somewhere west of Roswell. According to Lynn County historians Frank Hill and Pat Hill Jacobs, the miners opened a trail "between the two mining districts by way of Tahoka Lake" and Double Lakes.

"On one occasion," the Lynn County historians write, "a party of Mexicans had left the Croton mines with several burro loads of gold." When

Indians appeared, the men "hastily buried the gold in a grove of hackberry trees that once grew a short distance north of the lake." Hill and Jacobs reported that "a visitor to the Tahoka Lake shores today will find evidence of many excavations made by" people searching for the buried treasure.

In 1877, during the so-called Buffalo Soldier Tragedy of 1877, a remarkable event occurred at Guthrie Lake (but possibly Double Lakes). In June, after a heavy rainstorm, the lake covered about ten acres. Near the end of July, bison hunters and federal troops noted that the lake through absorption and evaporation had been reduced to five acres. Lieutenant Charles Cooper of the federal troops measured the lake's depth in its center at three feet.

The men "witnessed a remarkable sight," wrote one of the bison hunters, John Cook. "At one time during the day [July 23] could be seen horses, mules, buffaloes, antelopes, coyotes, wolves, a sand-hill crane, negro soldiers, white men, our part-Cherokee Indian and the Mexican guide [probably Jose Tafoya], all drinking and bathing at one and the same time from this lake."

Cook wrote that Cooper noted "outside of a tented circus, it was one of the greatest aggregations of the animal kingdom ever witnessed on as small a space of land and water." Cook also called attention to the high temperatures, constant sun on the water, "an occasional herd of buffalo standing and wallowing in it, plus "the ever-coming and going" of other animals and as a result the questionable quality of the water. "And yet," he wrote, "we mixed bread, made coffee, and filled our canteens from it." Six days later, after their scout for Indians had turned to disaster for lack of water, both soldiers and hunters, he concluded, "would have sold their birthright for the privilege of drinking and bathing in this same decoction."

Clearly, Lynn County's lakes and playas contain some remarkable history.

4

SILVER FALLS

PAUL H. CARLSON

For a few hundred years, the little cataracts and deep, narrow gorge along White River in Blanco Canyon at Silver Falls was used by Native Americans, Spanish and American explorers, comancheros, soldiers, cowboys, vacationers, university students, highway travelers and others.

The now shady place, located just east of Crosbyton, was and remains an inviting and relaxing location—although little water runs through it today. Unfortunately, officials built U.S. Highway 82 and Texas Highway 114 across the formerly sparkling spillway. Visitors must pull off the roadway to see the gentle cascades—during those few times when water is running.

Probably the earliest Native Americans in North America had visited and camped in the Silver Falls ravine before the first Spaniards showed up.

The conquering Spaniard Francisco Coronado did not see Silver Falls in 1541, but most of the participants in his huge expedition did. When Coronado took a handful of men out of Blanco Canyon and headed north to reach what today is south-central Kansas, his lieutenant, Captain Tristan de Arellano, led nearly 1,700 others with the expedition south to Silver Falls and then west through the northern reaches of present Lubbock and back to New Mexico, probably following either Yellow House or Blackwater Draw.

Comancheros, those New Mexican traders, for about a century (roughly 1786–1886) used the vicinity to stop, to rest and to exchange goods of all kinds with Indians, most notably Apaches and Comanches. Comancheros at first provided such foodstuffs as sugar and dried vegetables, as well as cloth, pots and pans, plus some other manufactured goods and tobacco. They later added watered-down alcohol and guns. Comanches provided dried meat, bison hides and robes and later added cattle.

In the last half of the nineteenth century, as the comanchero trade declined, Silver Falls became a more active place. In the 1870s, such American military leaders as Ranald Mackenzie of the Fourth Cavalry and his subaltern, William R. Shafter of the all-black Twenty-Fourth Infantry, several times camped near the falls with men of their regiments. One officer, Captain Theodore Baldwin of the all-black Tenth Cavalry, wrote to his wife in 1875 that in their Silver Falls camping area mosquitoes were "10,000 to the inch." Obviously, that summer, the Blanco River delivered an abundance of water over the falls and through its lightly wooded gulch.

Just upstream from the falls, Dewey Lake, another important landmark, attracted visitors. Early surveyors often camped at the lake, most often after 1876, when the legislature divided much of the Texas South Plains into counties. A group of surveyors marked out the Lubbock area in the summer of 1877, moved down Yellow House Canyon and then crossed over to Silver Falls before returning to Fort Worth. Texas Rangers maintained a station, called Camp Roberts, at the lake from 1879 until 1882. It was also the site of the Two-Buckle Ranch headquarters. Dewey Lake went dry in the 1880s when creeks eroded its banks, eventually draining away its water. According to a Texas Historical Commission marker near Silver Falls, "Remnants of Camp Roberts today are foundations of three sod buildings around an old well used by the Rangers."

Henry Clay "Hank" Smith, the famous first permanent Anglo settler on the South Plains, lived in Blanco Canyon several miles up White River from Silver Falls. He, his wife and children raised cattle and some sheep on their land, farmed it for hay for winter feed and put in a few fruit trees. The Smiths, with some of their neighbors, probably organized a few day outings to Silver Falls.

Other High Plains ranchers with their wives and cowboys went to Silver Falls on picnics. It was a grand place to rest from work, a place distinct and refreshing with a few trees, some shade from the relentless sun and cooling water. A large picnic was held there in 1911. As towns, such as Crosbyton and short-lived Emma and Estacado, appeared, villagers also made good use of Silver Falls for retreats, picnics and a good break from the monotony of High Plains life.

In the 1920s, a ranch owner, one of the various successors to the Two-Buckle, built a dam across White River at the upstream edge of the falls,

Long a favorite campsite for Native Americans, explorers and the military, picturesque Silver Falls became a popular picnic site. A gathering is shown in 1911. *Courtesy Southwest Collection, Texas Tech University.*

and the resulting lake behind the dam added to the attractiveness of the area. In 1926, freshmen students from Texas Technological College visited the place for a special outing and picnic. According to the Tech newspaper the *Toreador*, they did it again in 1927. The students boarded cars of the South Plains and Santa Fe Railroad Company in Lubbock and rode them to Crosbyton. From there, they walked or rode in horse-drawn wagons the three and a half miles to the camping area, where they fished and cavorted in the park-like setting.

Clearly, Silver Falls, with its refreshing water, its deep, steep-sided chasm, its general attractiveness and its easy reachable locale, made it for years a good place to stop and rest. It still is.

Part II

LAND AND LANDSCAPE

From ancient mammoths and camels to lobo wolves and prairie dogs, the Llano has hosted an abundance of exotic and common animals. For centuries, bison dominated the region, attracting not only human hunters but also large bands of migrating wolves. But it was the little prairie dog that outnumbered all wildlife and became a special challenge, especially for ranchers.

As you will see in the first essay, the Spanish description of a pool of water, *estancado*, may well be the term that later came to be understood as *estacado*. Regardless, whether it was the "pooled plains" or the "stockaded plains," water was—and is—extremely important to any who occupy the region. For example, another essay recalls how the military erected a monument—a lonely marker—to serve as a beacon to a nearby spring.

Producers of Tom Hanks's hit movie *Cast Away* chose for its closing scene the far northeastern part of the Llano Estacado, perhaps to compare the level plains, "an ocean of land," to the ocean from which Hanks's character had escaped. The scene from the film certainly captured the loneliness and isolation of that corner of the Llano, the same that the castaway experienced while on the small island in the Pacific.

5

Another Look at the Llano Estacado's Name

Meredith McClain

Over the years and since at least 1898, scholars have offered explanations of how we have derived the term *Estacado*. Does the name mean staked, palisaded, stockaded or something else?

Many people still suggest that the name came from the practice of Spaniards carrying stakes to plant in the ground to mark their way. Not true, of course, but it is hard to kill a myth.

Early Spaniards, such as Francisco Coronado and his scribes in the 1540s, used the forms *lo llano* or *el llano*, as in "y caminando para salir a lo llano" (and marching in order to cross the Plain). Or they wrote, "Los llanos proceden adelante, ni se sabe qué tanto" (The plains stretch away ahead nobody knows how far). They also wrote, "En estos llanos, que son como quien anda por el mar" (In these plains it was as if we had been swallowed up by the sea).

The late geographer John Miller Morris wrote that the word *estacado* was first used by ciboleros, New Mexican bison hunters. By the 1820s, they had an intimate knowledge of and great reverence, even love, for the Llano. Morris wrote, "They might have to do some maneuvering to get the buffalo on a good stretch of level ground suitable for a run. The amazing flatness of the Llano's vast tracts was in this sense a source of security, a crucial livelihood connection between the cibolero and his perception of the landscape."

Anglo-Americans, Morris suggested, were "forest men," familiar with trees, hills and mountains. They "found the horizontality [of the Plains] disturbing, [but] for the bison hunters it meant an exhilarating chase and less personal risk."

Early explorers on the Llano sometimes got lost and ran out of water. Only a few days after Coronado and his command were on the Llano, a hunter strayed away from the group and was lost, swallowed up by the sea, so to speak. Similar casualties occurred during the huge expedition's crossing of the Llano.

Coronado's Teyas guides made a few errors in leading the group, but they recovered the direction by arising early in the morning, orienting themselves to the sun and shooting arrows in the desired direction. At arrival of the arrows, they shot another load, and the command continued across the Plains.

After stopping in "Cona," present Blanco Canyon, Coronado divided his command. He sent the women and nearly all the men back, continuing with only a small group headed northeast to find the cities of gold he was after.

The Teyas guided the larger group (about 1,700 people) back to New Mexico. Pedro de Castañeda, an expedition scribe, reports that the guides moved "todo el día basta las aguas adonde se auia de hacer jornada" (all day long toward the waters whither they were to make camp). This group returned safely, camping each evening at a freshwater source (*hasta las aguas*). The Teyas knew the details of "la pista de agua viva" (trail of living water) across the Plains and the location of hidden ponds, the playas with drinkable water.

Castañedas noticed and carefully recorded the strange pools of water, round as plates (*lagunas redondas*), scattered all over the Llano. They are what we call today playa lakes (from the Spanish word for beach).

On the Llano in its early days of European use and occupation, we can be assured that the second-most important natural feature after its flatness—its horizontality—was water. Perhaps 50,000 playa lakes exist above the Ogallala Aquifer, with a majority of them (about 26,751) on the Llano.

Water in the playas and present along the upper streams (the trails of living water) of the Llano was essential to life on the high table land.

One need only read details of the Buffalo Soldier tragedy of 1877, the so-called Staked Plains Horror, to grasp the danger of missing sources of water on the Llano. In this instance missing water at the playas and along the upper streams resulted in four deaths and a demoralized, tortured company.

The playas, those shallow, circular ponds with no apparent opening to eliminate rainwater they collected, were relatively full in 1541 when Coronado crossed the Llano. His chief scribe, Castañeda, saw, studied and described them.

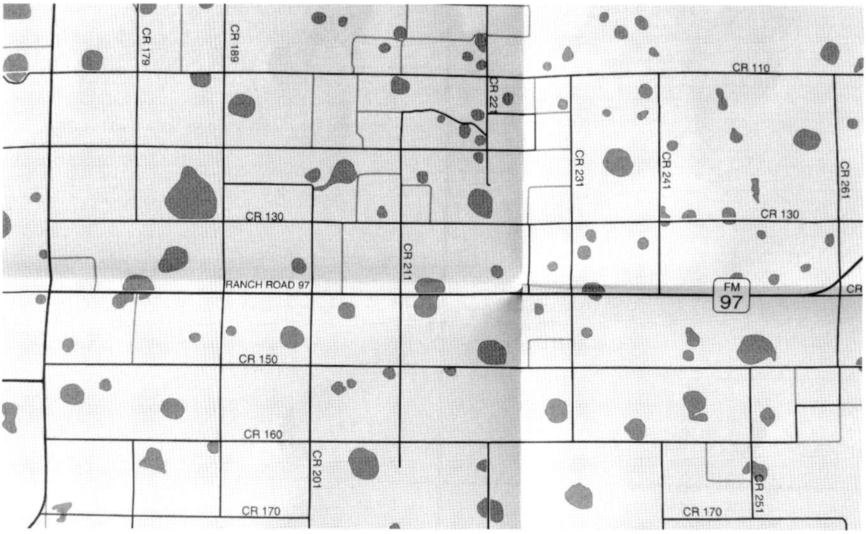

This map of a portion of Floyd County, Texas, shows the high concentration of playa lakes. More than eighteen thousand are located on the Llano Estacado. *Courtesy Floyd County Museum, Floydada, Texas, and Paul Carlson.*

The noun in Spanish for a still or stagnant pool is *estanque*. The adjectival form used to describe the playa/estanque formations on the Llano is *estancado*.

Clearly, then, El Llano Estancado (the pooled plain) is surely the original and explicit Mexican ciboleros' description of our locale, according to its definitive, ecological, most important two features, flat land of still ponds, and serves as a more precise definition of our great land form than other translations offered so far.

6

Prairie Dogs and Their "Towns"

Paul H. Carlson

The prairie dog," wrote Walter Prescott Webb, "is the squirrel of the Plains." He is partly correct. The prairie dog is a marmot, a rodent, related to the squirrel, and some of the first Anglo visitors to the western Plains compared them to squirrels—and to dogs.

Nearly all of us who live in West Texas know that prairie dogs, as Webb wrote, "inhabit the high, dry Plains and live in colonies, large or small." They eat grass, both the blades and roots; get by on little water; and rely primarily on their senses of sight and smell to warn of approaching danger.

Prairie dogs are good-natured, fairly clean and eminently social. But in the book *Raw Deal*, they are called the most hated animal in North America—hated even more than wolves and coyotes.

There are six species of prairie dogs. The black-tailed is most numerous in West Texas. They are seemingly everywhere. There are several colonies within the limits of Lubbock, especially along M.L. King Boulevard north of Twenty-Fourth Street; along the northeast loop of Highway 289; along Southeast Drive near Thirty-Fourth Street; and at the city-maintained Prairie Dog Town in Mackenzie Park. But City of Lubbock personnel have tried several times to remove prairie dogs from the city's gray-watered farms along east Fiftieth Street (Farm Road 835).

Once, prairie dogs numbered in the hundreds of millions on the Great Plains. Colonel Richard Irving Dodge of the U.S. Army wrote about them in 1877: "I regard the prairie dog as a machine designed by nature to convert

One of the thousands of prairie dogs that still inhabit the Llano Estacado east of Lubbock. *Courtesy Ellen Carlson.*

grass into flesh, and thus furnish proper food to the carnivore of the plains, which would undoubtedly soon starve but for the presence in such numbers of this little animal."

Cattlemen of the Old West did not like prairie dogs and saw them as a serious pest. Modern-day ranchers feel the same way. Horses and cattle step in prairie dog holes and break legs or sprain ankles, and prairie dogs eat grass that ranchers need as feed for livestock.

In 1905, Vernon Bailey, citing the *Yearbook of the United States Department of Agriculture* (1901), wrote, "they are found in scattered colonies or 'dog towns,' varying in extent from a few acres to a few square miles, but over an extensive area lying just east of the [Llano Estacado] they cover the whole country." Bailey described a prairie dog "town" that in 1901 extended from San Angelo north to Clarendon. The "thickly inhabited" and "almost continuous" colony covered "a strip approximately 100 miles wide by 250 miles long," or some 25,000 square miles. Agricultural officials estimated that the colony contained four hundred million prairie dogs.

In adjoining areas of West Texas, particularly on the High Plains, prairie dog towns in 1901 covered an additional 65,000 square miles for a total of

90,000 square miles of colonies in key livestock-grazing regions. According to the U.S. Agricultural Department, perhaps eight hundred million prairie dogs consumed enormous amounts of grass.

Figures in the 1901 Department of Agriculture publication suggest, Bailey writes, that this large "number of prairie dogs would require as much grass as 3,125,000 cattle." That number is wrong, experts have shown, but from a rancher's point of view, prairie dogs remain destructive animals.

But some prairie dogs, especially black-tails, make household pets. As early as the late eighteenth century, people were making domestic companions of them. A hundred years later, in 1877, a correspondent to *The Youth's Companion* wrote, "Our [prairie dog] village, which was started by the introduction of six or eight in our front yard, now consists of more than twenty funny little creatures, whose antics and gambols are equal to those of our own household pet, the kitten."

The correspondent indicated that the inquisitive little animals climbed into his lap and onto his shoulders, nibbled at the buttons on his shirt and searched for scraps of bed crumbs or crackers on his person, all while sniffing and chattering away.

In the 1890s, if the 1901 *Yearbook of Agriculture* is correct, prairie dogs in West Texas were increasing in number and spreading into new territory. The upsurge was due in part "to the destruction of their natural enemies, badgers, coyotes, foxes, ferrets, hawks, eagles, owls, and snakes."

Ranchers responded with poison—lots of it, and prairie dog populations weakened rapidly. A century later, with range habitat in decline, poison still in use and sport hunting now a popular method used to eliminate them, prairie dogs have become a threatened species. That is regrettable, for they are vital to maintaining a healthy Plains and prairie ecosystem.

Prairie dogs are still around—if not in such numbers as in 1901. They still live in colonies; they still eat plenty of grass; and, although to ranchers they remain destructive, to others they have become loveable pets.

7

Migrating Wolves

Paul H. Carlson and Ray Cragar

In February 1877, a rancher named John Lovelady, riding on horseback below the Caprock south of the mouth of Yellow House Canyon, witnessed thousands of wolves loping over the Plains and up the Yellow House.

The wolves, he said, were maybe "twenty abreast, and the pack must have been two or three miles in length." He saw them "heading in a northwestern course across the plains."

"On the same day," others wrote, "some parties [perhaps including William S. Glenn, a former bison hunter] saw what was undoubtedly this same pack crossing Yellow House Canyon, still traveling in a lope and headed northwest." A historical marker developed by Lubbock historian William C. Griggs and placed near the Lubbock Lake Site, commemorates the Lovelady-Glenn wolf sightings.

Such a migration had happened before 1877 and probably many times. David Lavender, in his scholarly book on William Bent's Fort in present Colorado, for example, relates a tale of migrating wolves. He writes about seventeen-year-old Bill Boggs, who, in 1844, was with a wagon train bound for Santa Fe through Bent's Fort. "One night," Lavender writes, near present-day Larned, Kansas, while Boggs stood "guard over…grazing mules, his heart leaped at the sound of a great splashing in the [Arkansas River]." He placed "his ear to the ground" and heard "the strangest rumbling, neither horses nor buffalo." Boggs soon "discovered a vast drove of migrating wolves." All night he "watched the ghostly packs plunge into" the wide Arkansas and paddle across—40,000 of them, he estimated (a number grossly inflated and one his sleeping companions ridiculed). The event occurred 430 miles north-northeast of Lubbock and thirty-three years before the Yellow House incident.

Lieutenant Robert G. Carter of the Fourth Cavalry also described large numbers of wolves. In *On the Border with Mackenzie*, he wrote that at night near a military camp on the Double Mountain Fork of the Brazos, near present-day Aspermont, in the early 1870s, wolves in countless numbers "came out of the 'bottoms' of numerous coulees, arroyos, and ravines."

"No such number of wolves," he wrote, "had ever been seen or heard by us in that country." In fact, "about the third or fourth night [in our camp] their number seemed to increase and double up." On the last night, he noted, the wolves "again congregated by thousands" and, thus, "we spent five days and nights in this wolf-besieged camp."

Clearly, in the past, wolves could be found in Texas in huge numbers. Indeed, the state was once home to several subspecies of gray wolf: Mexican gray wolf (in western portions of the state), Texas gray wolf (in central and south Texas) and the buffalo wolf (on the Plains following bison herds). Unfortunately, according to Jason Manning on the website Wolves: Wolf History, Conservation, Ecology and Behavior (wolfology/tripod.com), the Texas gray wolf became extinct about 1942. At one time, experts thought the buffalo wolf was extinct, but some subspecies may exist in the Michigan-Wisconsin area. The red wolf of eastern and central Texas is a separate wolf species.

Lieutenant Carter's wolves in the early 1870s were not leaving the Brazos River country, but Lovelady's and Glenn's wolves in 1877 and Boggs's animals in 1844 were migrating. What mysterious force caused them to congregate in such enormous numbers around Carter's camp or move in such massive totals along the Arkansas and Brazos rivers?

Wolf packs were rarely as sizeable as Carter, Lovelady and Boggs indicate their packs were. In the Lovelady and Boggs descriptions, particularly, the wolves moved as one colossal body strung out in wide formations and extending in length for miles. Clearly, at one time there were hundreds of thousands of gray (buffalo) wolves following the gigantic bison herds. Bison sometimes moved slowly, grazing along the way. Other times, they ran or stampeded in immense numbers and for long distances. Wolves followed, sometimes in smaller packs circling a quietly feeding herd of whatever size, and sometimes, as perhaps in the Boggs explanation of 1844, rushing to keep abreast of the animals they hunted.

Lobo wolves on the Llano Estacado. *Sketch by H.D. Bugbee, from the cover of* The Panhandle-Plains Historical Review *11 (1938). Used by permission.*

Plenty of questions remain, of course, especially about the 1877 wolf migration in our area. Where did they first congregate? Did one pack start the journey and others join along the way? If it was an "exodus" rather than a migration, what were they leaving behind, and where were they going?

Finally, did gray wolves really congregated in such astounding quantities? We know that bison numbers were huge, perhaps as many as twenty-five to thirty million during their peak years. But, in 1877, bison numbers in our area were in terrible decline. Also, cattlemen were pushing their livestock to and through former bison ranges toward our area, and the state had recently created more than fifty counties in the Panhandle–South Plains region.

Perhaps in response to such loss of prey and habitat, the buffalo wolves in inexplicable—and mysterious—ways still unknown to humans organized their hegira.

8

Monument Spring

Paul H. Carlson

One of the unique sites on the Llano Estacado featured a short-lived but notable structure built by federal soldiers in 1875. Intended to be a beacon to mark the location of a nearby flowing spring, the pillar quickly became known as a monument.

Monument Spring in southeastern New Mexico served Native Americans, explorers, soldiers, travelers and area residents. The crossroads village of Monument, about twelve miles southwest of Hobbs, is named for the spring and a no-longer-extant stone and rock monument built by U.S. soldiers in the summer of 1875 to help locate the spring during future operations.

Lieutenant Colonel William R. Shafter of the Twenty-Fourth Infantry, an African American regiment, ordered the monument built on a rise of land above the spring. When finished, the monument was eight feet wide at the base and four feet at the top. It stood seven and a half feet high, and in the treeless region, it could be seen for miles.

Shafter and his troops in the long, hot summer of 1875 had been searching the Llano Estacado for several months. Their orders were to locate Indians, especially Comanches, remaining on the Llano after the Red River War in the Texas Panhandle and return them to their reservations. In addition, they were to explore the high tableland, which was still seen as something of a mysterious place that cattlemen and travelers avoided, and Shafter was to note its potential for cattle raising.

Shafter's men covered the region from Tule Canyon south to the Rio Grande. They discovered waterholes previously unknown to the Anglo world and explored Indian and bison trails, but they found only a few Indians—Apaches—near Cedar Lake, the largest body of water, although alkaline, on the Llano Estacado, and near Monument Spring.

Officers and soldiers of the Twenty-Fourth Infantry and Tenth Cavalry—another black regiment—followed the Pecos River south but stopped at Horsehead Crossing. After resting a few days, the command backtracked upriver to Pecos Falls and from there proceeded northeastward toward the lower end of the Monahans Sand Hills, looking for the Apaches others had flushed at Cedar Lake.

The hunt was rewarded. On September 9, near modern-day Odessa, Shafter's scouts struck an Indian trail. Pursuing it westward eight miles, they discovered an abandoned camp that had contained one hundred families and a large horse herd. The main command joined the chase and followed Indian tracks to water holes at the upper end of the Sand Hills, where it rested and watered horses. After midnight, the men rode northwestward until sunrise, when they rested two hours before continuing. As water supplies disappeared, pursuit proved impossible; thirst, dust and heat took a heavy toll on men and animals.

On the twelfth, advance troops located another spring where the Indians had stopped. Prospects of catching the elusive Apaches brightened, and Shafter brought the main body of his troops to the water hole. Here, at Three Wells—or Dug Spring, as Shafter called it in his report—the Indians took the offensive. At 2:00 a.m., a party of thirty Apache warriors struck the camp but scattered when guards returned the fire. The only losses were four horses the Indians captured. At dawn, Shafter, with forty-five picked troops, went after the Apaches.

Twenty miles to the north, at the large water hole that he later called Monument Spring, Shafter found a recently abandoned Apache camp. Upon bringing up the main command, he ordered all lodges and other camp equipage at the isolated sanctuary destroyed. The work took several hours.

Shafter also sent troops to build a rock monument on a low hill about a mile and a quarter to the southwest of the water hole. He wanted a large marker to show the location of the spring. Building the solid structure was not easy work. The men gathered large white stones and rocks from the area and placed them at the top of the hill.

After his men finished building the tall marker and destroying the large camp, Shafter gave up the chase for the Apaches. His rations were low,

This ranch house, located a few miles west of Monument, New Mexico, sits just below the rise where soldiers built a monument in 1875 and is constructed in part from its stones. *Courtesy David Murrah.*

his animals were worn and the Indians had scattered in all directions. On September 16, he headed back across the Llano to Blanco Canyon and his home base.

The monument stood for many years. The site and its abundant spring became the headquarters of the vast Hat Ranch. The early cattlemen and homesteaders after the turn of the century used stones and rocks from the structure to build their homes. The big marker slowly crumbled. Then, in the mid-twentieth century, as the huge Permian oil field opened up, well drillers used caterpillar tractors—bulldozers—to level the top of the low hill where the monument had been erected.

No sign of the marker exists today. But it is remembered in the name of the tiny village of Monument, New Mexico, located nearby, the spring there that bears its name and the military reports and history books that cover the 1875 Shafter expedition across the Llano Estacado. It is also commemorated at a fine display in the Western Heritage Center and Lea County Hall of Fame in Hobbs, New Mexico.

9

Cast Away and the Texas Panhandle's Arrington Ranch

Paul H. Carlson

The wonderful beginning and closing scenes of the popular 2000 movie *Cast Away*, starring Tom Hanks and Helen Hunt, were filmed in Hemphill County of the West Texas Panhandle near Canadian, far up in the eastern-northeastern Panhandle.

The final scenes, which symbolize a man at a crossroads in his life, occurred in the extreme southwest corner of Hemphill County where Farm to Market Road 48, Farm to Market Road 1268 and County Road 5 meet. The lonely corner is southeast of Miami and southwest of Canadian, Texas. At the close of the movie, Hanks, as the film's leading character Chuck Noland, turns and looks briefly from the middle of the intersection in each direction. In all four directions the road reaches straight to a vanishing point on the far horizon.

Here is a scene, if not typical, at least characteristic of the West Texas Panhandle: empty land and open space stretching as far as the eye can see.

In fact, by a more than century-old government definition, the area is something of a modern frontier. That is to say, in 1890, the federal government classified a region with less than two people per square mile as a "frontier." In the Texas Panhandle, Roberts County in 2020 held fewer than nine hundred people, less than one person per square mile. Under the federal government's erstwhile definition, Briscoe and Oldham counties also qualify as frontier. Several others, including Collingsworth, Hartley, Lipscomb, Sherman and Hemphill, remain barely removed from frontier status.

In a transcendental way, the Hemphill County location in the closing scene of *Cast Away* is a beautiful, unblemished spot. There is romance and melancholy about the place, and in 2020, no ranch house, no barn or shed and no clump of trees break the wide view of space and sky and ever-changing clouds.

In the 1830s, George Catlin, who toured the Plains to record Indian life and customs, noted that the region was "a place where the mind could think volumes; but the tongue must be silent that would *speak*, and the hand palsied that would *write*."

With passion, the sometimes mulish Kiowa leader Satanta in 1867 described his feelings for the region. "I love the land," he said, "I love to roam over the wide prairie...and when I do, I feel free and happy."

North from the lonely, isolated intersection, presumably the direction Chuck Noland planned to take, along the caliche-based County Road 5, is George and Jane Arrington's ranch. The Arrington Ranch, in the Arrington family for more than 125 years, is owned and operated by Mike, Debbie and their three sons and their families. The Arringtons live in Canadian. Their son Mike handles responsibilities associated with the ranch.

The Arrington Ranch House, located five miles northeast of Miami, Texas, sits on the far northeastern edge of the Llano Estacado and was used in the closing scene of the movie *Cast Away*. *Courtesy Arrington Ranch House Lodge, Canadian, Texas.*

Mike and his wife once operated a bed-and-breakfast at the old headquarters home, then called the Arrington Ranch House Lodge. It is located about five and a half miles north of the out-of-the-way intersection, and it can be seen twice in *Cast Away*. The home was built in 1918 by Mike's great-grandfather George Washington "Cap" Arrington, who bought the land from the state of Texas. The Arrington home is used for resting in comfort for overflow of family and friends.

Cap Arrington was a Confederate veteran from Alabama and later a Texas Ranger. He had come to Texas from Honduras sometime after shooting to death a black businessman in 1867. After changing his name from John C. Orrick Jr., Arrington joined the Rangers and served in South Texas. In 1879, he became captain of Company C of the Frontier Battalion, and officials in Austin sent him to the Texas Panhandle. Although effective, Arrington was a stern and aggressive officer who made enemies as easily as he made friends.

He resigned his captaincy in 1882. He became a rancher and served as sheriff of Wheeler County and fourteen as yet unorganized counties that were administratively and judiciously attached to it.

Arrington, who married Sarah "Sally" Caroline Burnette in 1883, lived in Mobeetie while he was sheriff of Wheeler County. The couple had nine children. They left Mobeetie in 1891, when Arrington resigned as sheriff. They moved to their ranch along the upper Washita River and its tributaries in Hemphill County about fifteen miles north of town.

In 1893, British owners of the 250,000-acre Rocking Chair Ranche, which was headquartered in Collingsworth County, asked Arrington to manage their land and cattle company. He agreed. Three years later, the Englishmen sold their property, and Arrington returned to his own ranch. Cap Arrington died in 1923.

The Arrington Ranch remains in the family. Except for the trees and shrubs, not much has changed. In 2017, the Arrington Ranch House Lodge; the entry drive with its tall, colorful archway; and the wide barn out back remained remarkably as they did in *Cast Away*, the twenty-year-old movie with some dramatically characteristic scenes of the West Texas Panhandle.

Part III

EXPLORATION AND TRAGEDY

Without knowledge of a permanent source of water, the early explorers of the Llano Estacado proved to be fearless in their efforts to traverse the inhospitable Plains. From the Coronado Expedition in 1540–41 to the Buffalo Soldier Tragedy in 1877, searching for water often became the unintentional objective of every foray.

Virtually every Spanish and American exploration effort struggled to find water, but the native Apache, Kiowa, Cheyenne and Comanche peoples, who had crisscrossed the region many times in following the bison herds, knew of the infrequent springs and the *la pista de agua viva*, the mysterious trail of living water that remained undiscovered by Anglo explorers almost to modern times.

In the midst of exploration of the Llano, conflict between native people and soldiers/hunters led to two separate tragedies in 1877.

10

Francisco Amangual and the Upper Brazos River

Paul H. Carlson

Don Francisco Amangual (1739–1812), a Spanish cavalry soldier and later officer of distinction, served Spain in a number of regions in America, including Sonora, before an assignment in 1874 took him to San Antonio.

In Texas, Amangual shifted duty stations between the presidios San Antonio de Bexar and Nuestra Senora de Loreto (La Bahia), pursued Comanches, guarded the coast against a supposed "invasion" of Texas by the American spy Philip Nolan and handled administrative functions at the presidios.

On March 30, 1808, Amangual, almost seventy years old, led some two hundred men out of San Antonio and headed for Santa Fe with the expressed purpose of finding a shorter route between the two Spanish outposts. The need for a shorter road stemmed from two developments. In response to Napoleon Bonaparte's takeover of their country, Spanish leaders in Mexico City sought to hold on to their empire in the New World. To help do that, they wanted a quicker route between their major outposts in the Southwest.

At the same time, officials in Mexico City worried about an exploring party in the Southwest led by American soldier Lieutenant Zebulon Pike two years earlier. They wanted to impress Americans with the power and mobility of the Spanish military.

Most historians suggest that Captain Amangual's route went from San Antonio to the Llano Estacado's eastern Caprock and followed it north before heading west by way of present-day Amarillo. If so, nothing new was accomplished. Other historians, including the influential H. Bailey Carroll, argue for a path via the upper Brazos River through present-day Lubbock—an upper Brazos River route.

Carroll cites Amangual's translated diary for May 1808. If Carroll is correct, on May 19, somewhere near the mouth of Yellow House Canyon below modern-day Slaton, Amangual wrote that, from the High Plains, "We descended to a creek bottom covered with gravel…and we continued to go up and down slight elevations until we…reached an extensive canyon which is formed by a rim of hills to the west." The water was fresh, noted Amangual, and the creek "flows from northwest to southeast." They followed it.

The next day, May 20, the Spanish captain wrote in his diary, "The bluffs of the canyon are not very high; they are generally red, but in places, streaked with white." He noted that they "found a spring of water and a beautiful cave so large that twelve men could stand in the entrance." Professor Carroll believed the cave was located somewhere between modern Slaton and Buffalo Springs Lake. "The interior of the cave, which was narrow, was all painted with various colors and figures by the Indians."

In the canyon, the explorers followed "along the banks of the river, which were thickly covered with poplars. A small creek flowing some water joined the river." The site may be either where Pig Squeal Creek in modern-day Ransom Canyon joins the Yellow House or where Yellow House and Blackwater draws meet in present Mackenzie Park. Amangual and his men camped at the watery place with its grass- and tree-lined banks.

On May 21, the diary reads, "We again set out on our way along the same canyon, which was quite narrow, with rocky ledges on both sides…and with several exceedingly uncomfortable bluffs." They traveled only nine miles "this day." On the twenty-second, they "remained in camp until noon." Amangual planned to leave the canyon and ordered his men to prepare for a long afternoon march across the Plains to "a point from which we would reach a water-hole tomorrow."

On setting out, they left "behind the rims that form the canyon [and] began to travel over plains so immense that the eye could not see their end. There was nothing but grass and a few small pools of rain water." They "found a few pools of rain water, with very little water, and some dry holes." Because there were no trees, Amangual wrote, "Where we camped it was necessary to drive pins for the guard and reserve horses. Nothing hindered the travel."

The expedition reached Santa Fe without further difficulty. On December 23, having gone by way of El Paso, its members returned to San Antonio.

Francisco Amangual mentioned seeing a cave in Yellow House Canyon similar to this one. *Courtesy Paul Carlson.*

Amangual's accomplishment, if in fact he came up Yellow House Canyon and Blackwater Draw, changed in no significant way circumstances for the Spanish empire in the Southwest. An independence movement against Spain, now under French control, began in 1810, and a decade later, Mexico gained self-rule.

Upon his return to San Antonio in 1808, Don Francisco Amangual retired. He died two years later.

11
THE COMANCHE WAR TRAIL

PAUL H. CARLSON

The historian and lively storyteller J. Evetts Haley called it the "Great Comanche War Trail." It was a 'broad highway," he wrote, "that skirted the" Llano Estacado. It carried Comanches south into Mexico. It lasted for nearly one hundred years, becoming a well-worn trail.

In 1854, while crossing West Texas, U.S. Army officer John Pope, writes Haley, "was astonished by the heavy traffic" near Mustang Springs "that had beaten out this great trail."

One arm of the great trail began in Indian Territory and southern Kansas. It "took a course that [moved south] passed the western extremity of the Wichita Mountains." A second arm traced south from the upper Arkansas River and crossed the Canadian River and the upper reaches of the Red east of the Caprock escarpment. The arms converged along the White River below where its waters gushed from Blanco Canyon. Remaining just east of the Caprock, the trail moved to Big Spring and then split at Sulphur Springs near the lower end of Sulphur Draw.

From there, in the upper Concho River country, there were several arms and/or subdivisions. An eastern branch trailed south across the Edwards Plateau to follow Los Moras Creek and the upper Nueces River to Mexico. A western branch moved past the White Sand Hills near present-day Monahans and forded the Pecos River at Horsehead Crossing. It ran by Comanche Springs and Leon Water Hole before entering the Big Bend. The western branch forked somewhere near

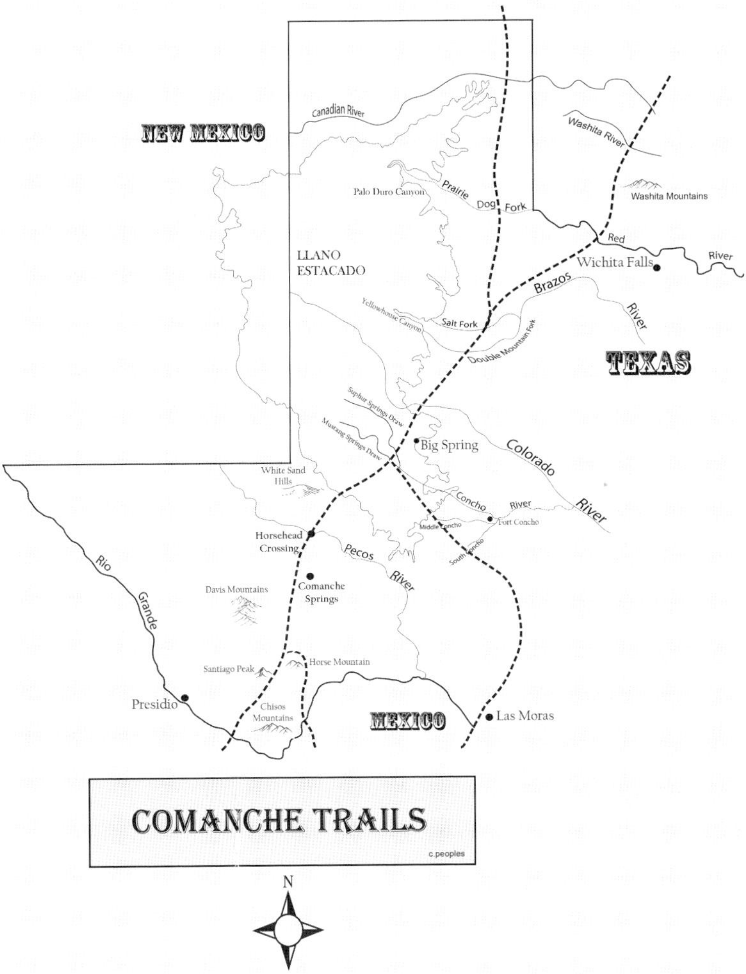

The main branch of the Comanche War Trail skirted around the southeast quadrant of the Llano Estacado and generally followed the route of present U.S. Highway 83 along the east side of the Panhandle. *Courtesy Curtis Peoples, based on an earlier map by Jose Cisneros.*

what Haley calls "the Camel Hump or Horse Mountain," with one route crossing the Rio Grande near Lajitas.

Another route, "the main trail," as Haley calls it, "kept to the left of Horse Mountain," and went "south through Persimmon Gap." It "crossed the Rio Grande…at what was called 'The Grand Indian Crossing'," near modern-day Boquillas, Mexico.

If Texas and Comanche historian Rupert Richardson is correct, the Comanche forays into Mexico began in the late eighteenth century. They increased after a treaty between Comanches and Spanish authorities in 1785 allowed villagers from New Mexico (comancheros) to enter the Plains east of the Pecos River to trade with Indians. Trading sites existed up and down the eastern Caprock.

The incursions were often large and always destructive expeditions, and Kiowas and Apaches also followed the trails. Over time, Indian warriors struck deep into Mexico and over a wide area. Haley describes their raiding methods as "a war of movement," bringing "terror, pillage and devastation" to towns, villages, ranches and great haciendas across Durango, Zacatecas and Chihuahua.

The Indians, according to Pope, "carry into captivity hundreds of human beings, and thousands of horses and mules." Richardson stated that Mexican citizens estimated 652 people "killed, wounded, or captured in the state of Nuevo Leon from 1847 to 1857."

By the 1830s, the Comanche assaults had become serious enough to be the subject of negotiations between the United States and Mexico. In the 1840s and early 1850s, the raids reached a peak in number of strikes, harm to Mexican citizens and destruction of property.

In 1846, English adventurer George F. Ruxton, while passing through northern Mexico, was present at Hacienda La Noria in Durango when Comanches were spotted. A warning was sounded, he said, and everybody was "in greatest alarm and dismay....The women were weeping and flying about in every direction, hiding their children and valuables, barricading the houses, and putting what few arms they could collect into the hands of the reluctant men."

A year later, in 1847, during the U.S. war with Mexico, the noted Comanche headman Buffalo Hump gathered about seven hundred warriors to enter Mexico. According to Haley, he planned to strike Chihuahua City on his way south and perhaps San Antonio on his return.

The Indians usually carried their captives, stolen livestock and other spoils back along the same route as they entered Mexico. Comancheros, especially, but perhaps other traders as well, awaited them at favorite sites, including Mushaway Peak in present Borden County or Yellow House, Blanco, Quitaque, Los Lingos and Palo Duro canyons. There were plenty of trading sites. And in the 1850s and afterward, comancheros were often supported by American businessmen in Santa Fe and Las Vegas who wanted cattle—large numbers of them to deliver to towns and mining camps in the Rocky Mountains.

Comanche, as well as Apache and Kiowa, raids into Mexico declined for several reasons. The U.S. Army began to build forts at significant waterholes, such as Comanche Springs (Fort Stockton), along the trail. Indians entered reservation life. An advancing Texas population spread into West Texas. And "scalp hunters" spread across northern Mexico to intercept raiders from north of the Rio Grande.

By then, the trail, as one historian has written, "worn deep by the hoofs of countless travelers, man and beast, and whitened by the bones of animals," passed into history.

12

Buffalo Soldiers on the Llano Estacado

Paul H. Carlson

For half a decade in the 1870s, black troopers (Buffalo Soldiers) of the U.S. Army rode across the Llano Estacado.

The African American troopers chased American Indians, particularly Apaches, Comanches and Cheyennes; scouted the high, empty plateau, mapping it and opening roads across it; located important water holes; and participated in the event-changing Red River War of 1874–75.

Segregated black military units, especially infantry, had been created near the end of the American Civil War. After the war in 1866, the U.S. Army established several permanent black companies, but reorganization three years later produced the Ninth and Tenth Cavalry regiments (both all-black divisions led by white officers) and two black infantry groups, the Twenty-Fourth and Twenty-Fifth regiments.

The cavalry regiments were known to Indians as "Buffalo Soldiers." But, because Indians seldom distinguished between infantry and cavalry divisions (in fact, the infantry was often mounted in the Southwest), all-black troops came to be called by the storied sobriquet.

Black soldiers were volunteers. They were usually single and about twenty-three to twenty-six years old. The army mainly recruited them from eastern states of the Upper South with such cities as Baltimore, Washington, Chattanooga and Wilmington providing many of the recruits.

Between 1870 and 1875, the Tenth Cavalry and the Twenty-Fourth Infantry especially served on the Llano Estacado. For thirty-five days in

August and September 1870, Buffalo Soldiers scoured the Llano's southern fringe. In the vicinity of the Pecos and headwaters of the Llano rivers, they discovered a favorite Indian camping place, found water holes previously unknown, caught eight Apache ponies and demonstrated that Indians would no longer be able to use the place as a safe rendezvous.

A year later, black soldiers spent twenty-two days in torrid heat exploring the White Sand Hills near present-day Monahans. They followed trails through the shifting hills and onto the Llano Estacado to a point southwest of modern Hobbs, New Mexico, and thence southwestward to the Pecos.

In the summer of 1872, some 177 soldiers of the Twenty-Fourth Infantry joined Ranald S. Mackenzie, one of the army's most successful officers, in Blanco Canyon. From there, Buffalo Soldiers protected the main camp, called Camp Supply, and scouted some of the canyons and breaks of the eastern Caprock. Mackenzie led other troopers across the Llano Estacado to Fort Sumner in New Mexico and back. By the close of the summer campaign, black cavalrymen had mapped the Llano west to Fort Sumner, noted several sources of water, explored thoroughly the Double Mountain Fork of the Brazos River and gained valuable knowledge needed for later military operations.

In 1873, federal military operations in Texas shifted to the Rio Grande border, where soldiers, including some black troops, crossed into Mexico to stop Kickapoo and Lipan Apache raids into Texas.

The army temporarily ignored the Llano Estacado. Then, in 1874, after Comanches, under their young leader Quanah, and Cheyennes attacked bison hunters along the Canadian River, the U.S. Army returned. In the largest concentration of troops on the Southern Plains, soldiers, including Buffalo Soldiers of the Tenth Cavalry, struck Indians in the Panhandle. They attacked from five directions.

When fighting, called the Red River War, ended in late winter and early spring 1875 and most Indians had returned to their reservations, Buffalo Soldiers searched the Llano Estacado for holdouts from the hostilities.

For six months from June to December, black soldiers crisscrossed the Llano Estacado over a veritable maze of trails, covering 2,500 miles of the High Plains between the eastern Caprock and the Pecos River. Their expedition represented the most thorough exploration of the Llano Estacado to that time. They marked water holes, opened roads, noted fuel supplies, recorded flora and fauna and mapped the region. They found only four Indians, three Apache women and a child. No one had done more to dispel the longstanding desert myth of the Llano than men and officers of the Tenth and Twenty-Fourth regiments.

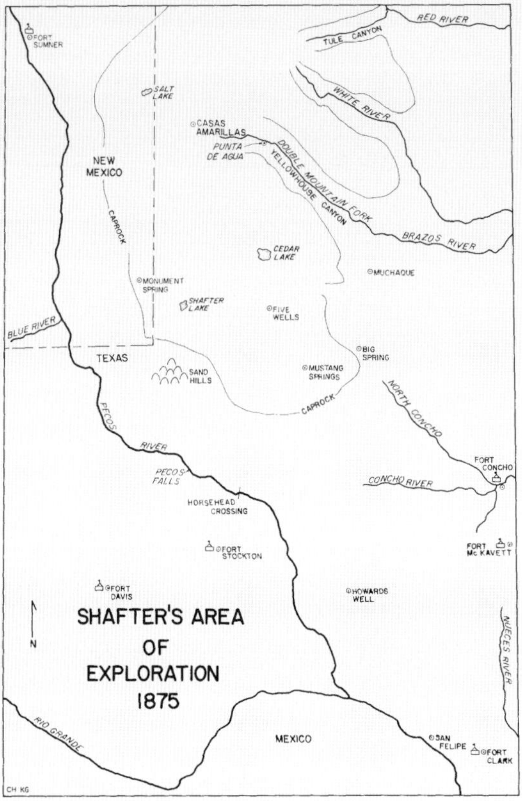

Left: Troops under William R. Shafter left from Fort Concho (*lower right*) to explore this vast region in the summer of 1875. *Map from* "Pecos Bill:" A Military Biography of William R. Shafter *by Paul H. Carlson*.

Below: These Buffalo Soldiers were in Company A of the Tenth Cavalry. *Courtesy Institute of Texan Cultures, San Antonio, Texas*.

Clearly, Buffalo Soldiers played a powerful role in the opening of the Llano Estacado. Elsewhere, they may have guarded mail routes, rode shotgun on stagecoaches, built telegraph lines and constructed buildings. But not on the Llano. On the Llano Estacado, they were explorers. They searched the large region's borderlands and thoroughly reconnoitered, mapped and recorded its topographical features.

They connected by wagon roads previously unknown water holes on the Plains with well-known trails. They observed the extreme western range of bison herds and noted the region's excellent potential for ranching and farming.

Perhaps most important, on the Llano Estacado they paved the way for an advancing white population, and indeed, in 1876, Charles Goodnight trailed a large herd of cattle from Colorado onto the Southern Plains and into Palo Duro Canyon. Anglo settlement had begun.

13

Massacre at Silver Lake

Paul H. Carlson

On May 4, 1877, black soldiers of Troop G, Tenth Cavalry, struck a small Comanche camp at Silver Lake, located south of modern-day Pep and northeast of present-day Morton, killing at least four people and capturing six women.

The encounter came late in the long series of soldier-Indian fights on the Llano Estacado, and it came against Comanches, some of whom with passes were off their reservation in Indian Territory to hunt. The fight, or massacre as it has been called, grew from Anglo bison hunter activities in West Texas in 1876 and 1877. For two years, bison hunters had been striking herds across the large prairie-plains region west of Fort Griffin in Shackelford County.

The hunters sought bison hides, and they proved enormously successful, killing large numbers of the animals. They stripped hides from the dead animals and left the carcasses to wolves, coyotes, turkey vultures, ravens and scavengers of all kinds.

Indians, especially Comanches, while hunting off their reservations found the rotting carcasses, sometimes one hundred or more within a few-acres stand. Angry with what was happening in their hunting reserve, Comanches attacked bison hide men; destroyed their camps; and burned their wagons, equipment and supplies. Sometimes, they killed a hunter or his hide-skinning aides.

Bison hunters complained to local officials and to the federal army. Sometimes, they organized expeditions against Comanches, as in March

1877, when they and Indians fought the inconclusive battle of Yellow House Canyon in today's Lubbock area. The army also sent troopers into the field after Comanches, Apaches or others who were attacking the bison hunters. A detachment of Troop I, Tenth Cavalry, from Fort Richardson covered over one thousand miles in an unsuccessful effort to locate Comanches.

A second expedition led to the massacre. On April 9, muscular and square-shouldered Captain Phillip Lee, Troop G, Tenth Cavalry, left Fort Griffin with six Tonkawa scouts and seventy-two men of his command. Lee and his black soldiers stopped briefly at Rath City, a booming bison-hide trade center near the Double Mountain Fork of the Brazos River in Stonewall County, before heading west to the Llano Estacado to find, punish and return Indians to their reservations.

Nearly a month later, on May 4, Lee and his troopers found a camp at Silver Lake (Laguna Plata, sometimes called Lake Quemado or simply Quemos) and struck hard. As indicated, they killed four people and seized six others. Among the dead, wrote one of the Comanches later, was Batsena, "a very brave warrior," whose body the Tonkawa scouts scalped and mutilated. Also among the dead was Batsena's "daughter, Nooki, a beautiful Indian maiden, who [was] disemboweled and scalped."

Herman Lehman, an Anglo who had become a Comanche warrior, later wrote that when he and other young men returned to Silver Lake from a horse-stealing venture along the upper San Saba River, they found bodies "horribly mangled" and camp equipage wrecked or missing. We "soon found our scattered women and children and old men," Lehman remembered, "and heard the sad details of the attack." Everyone was "badly demoralized," but before seeking revenge, they determined to reorganize—"to get our forces together and move to another part of the country." They headed west into sand hills in eastern New Mexico.

Meanwhile, the troopers, who had suffered one dead (Sergeant Charles Baker) themselves, had rounded up sixty-nine horses, burned tipis and destroyed most supplies and camp equipage. They placed Baker's body in a grave they dug in a creek bed, and they buried a few hundred pounds of lead that Comanches planned to use for bullets. Neither the grave nor the lead has been found.

On their return to Fort Griffin, Lee (perhaps a relative of Civil War general Robert E. Lee) and his troops again stopped at Rath City. There they rested a bit. They also reported the results of their engagement at Silver Lake to bison hunters at the trade center and distributed some of the horses, which Comanches had stolen earlier, to hide men and area cowboys.

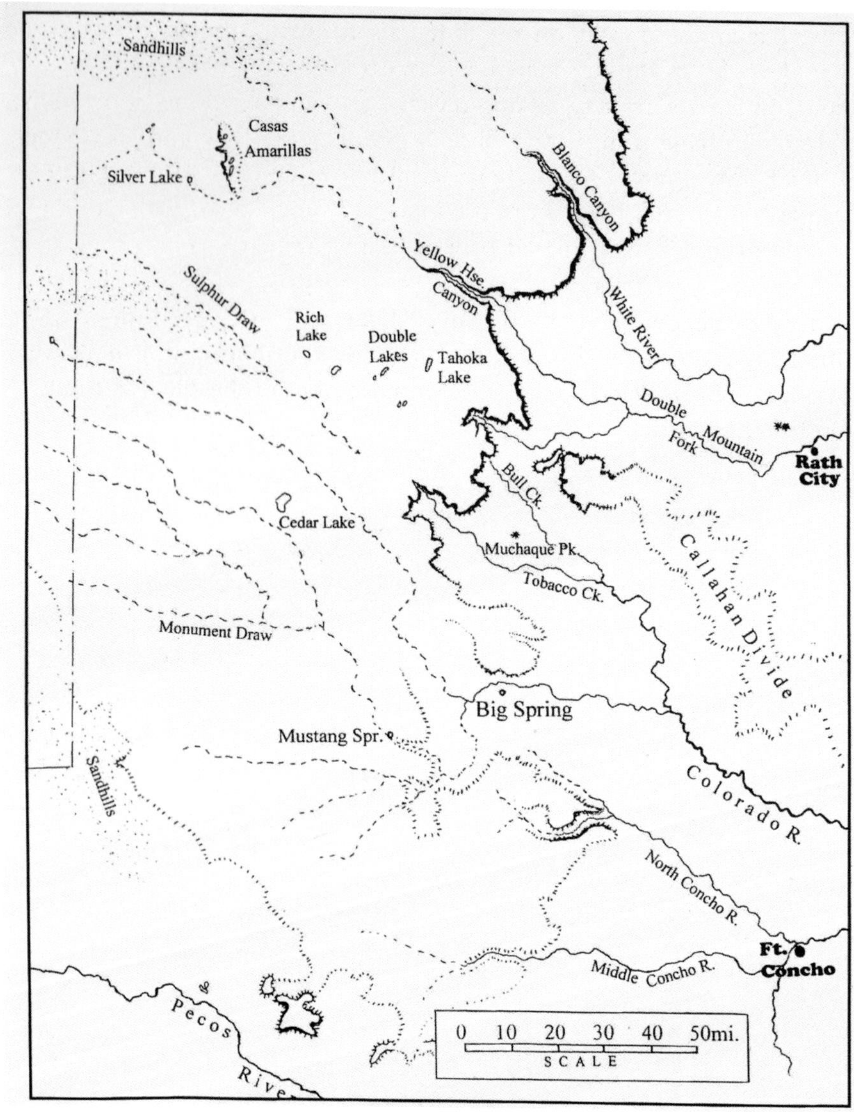

This map shows Silver Lake and Rath City in relation to other points of the Llano Estacado. Even though the two places were more than 150 miles apart, the Silver Lake battle tied them together. *Map by Michael Harter; courtesy Paul Carlson.*

Lee's favorable report on the fight raised spirits. Thinking the region was safe, a few bison hunters once more turned to the range. They were wrong. Indiana warriors, seeking revenge and an end to the bison killing, again hit outlying camps. And, shortly after Captain Lee and his troopers left Rath City, a group of perhaps seventy-five warriors struck Rath City in a pre-dawn raid. They shot up the place, stole more than one hundred horses and mules and hurried back to their camps deep on the western edge of the Llano Estacado.

Clearly, the deadly fight at Silver Lake did not end Indian–bison hunter antagonism. Raids and counterraids continued until there were not enough bison left to make hide procurement profitable and the hide men left the range.

14

The Staked Plains Horror

Paul H. Carlson

In the eighteenth and nineteenth centuries, the Llano Estacado could be a brutal country. The high tableland with its relentless winds, semi-arid climate, monotonous terrain and mercurial temperatures mystified visitors. July 1877 was no different.

This time, a party of twenty-two bison hunters and some forty men of the Tenth Cavalry—Buffalo Soldiers—with their white officers and a guide on July 26 left Double Lakes, twenty-five miles south of present-day Lubbock, in pursuit of a band of Comanche warriors. Heading in a northwest direction, the hunters and soldiers soon ran out of water, lost their way, argued over the route to follow and, somewhere northeast of present-day Morton, went separate ways. Both groups writhed in pain.

By mid-July, the hide men, twenty-four in number and led by army veteran Jim Harvey, had been on the Llano Estacado, or "Yarner," for two months searching for stolen horses. At the time, they were in camp just off the eastern Caprock in the Muchaque Peak country near modern Gail in Borden County, planning a return to the high Llano.

The soldiers, led by Captain Nicolas Nolan, had ridden out of Fort Concho on July 10. With sixty men and four six-mule wagons to carry supplies, they headed north to locate Comanches and get them back to the reservation. A week later, they rode into the bison hunter camp. After a short parley, the hunters and soldiers joined forces. The hunters agreed to serve as guides. The soldiers would do any fighting that might occur.

Captain Nicholas Nolan. His bad decisions led to what newspapers called the "Staked Plains Horror." *Courtesy Lesle Nash Loughridge.*

Two days later, on July 19, they pulled out of the grassy, well-watered camp along Bull Creek. Nolan's soldiers left behind the wagons and twenty men, as the site would serve as the base of operations. Two bison hunters also stayed behind to look after equipment and wagons belonging to the hide men. A week later, after some misadventures, the combined command was in camp at Double Lakes in Lynn County when two bison hunters, who had been scouting for Indian signs, rode in to report the location of a fresh trail.

The pursuit was on. The fresh trail they followed zigzagged in a northwest direction as Comanches, realizing they were being followed, tried to lose their pursuers. They were successful. Moreover, and unfortunately, temperatures stood above one hundred degrees and many of the playas had dried up. Inexplicitly, some of the soldiers, busy with army details, forgot or had no chance to fill their canteens or water containers.

The first night, July 26, soldiers and hunters made a dry camp somewhere in extreme southwest Hockley County just above Sulphur Draw. As expedition members began running out of water, hunters shared with soldiers what liquid remained in their canteens. The next day, July 27, under a broiling sun, out of water and with several soldiers suffering from sunstroke, they crossed through Cochran County but gave up the chase.

After still another dry camp, this one just over the border in New Mexico, command leaders set a course for Silver Lake, thirty miles to the east on the present Cochran-Hockley County line and the Casas Amarillas basin north of present Levelland, where water was available. About midday on July 28, Nolan again decided to change course. He split from the hunters and led his soldiers back toward Double Lakes. It was a major mistake.

As planned, the bison hunters headed for Silver Lake. Without water under the hot, relentless sun, they endured extreme hardship. Disoriented, dehydrated and suffering, they split into small groups. Some found relief at the lake; others reached water in Casas Amarillas.

The Buffalo Soldiers were not so fortunate. As they moved toward Double Lakes without water, they could not eat. Sunstroke increased, men fell

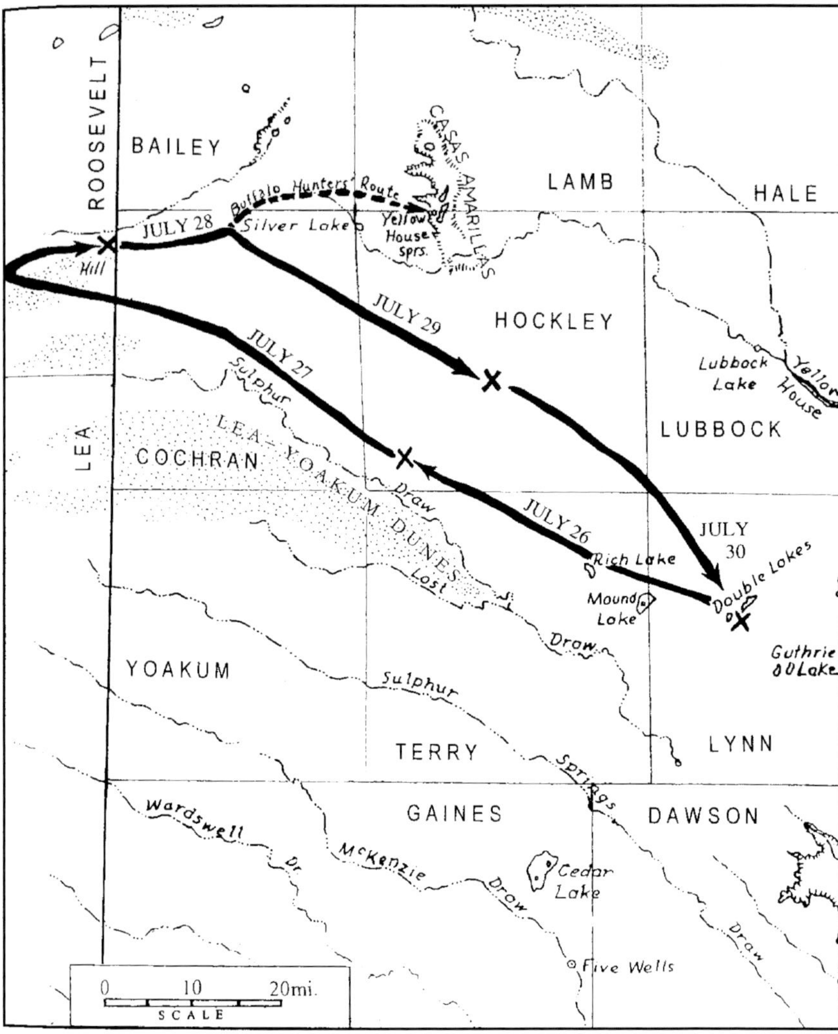

This was the route taken by Buffalo Soldiers and bison hunters in July 1877, traversing one of the longest waterless stretches of the Llano Estacado. *Map by Michael Harter, courtesy Paul Carlson.*

behind, some deserted and some just disappeared. As their horses gave out, putting the men on foot, they abandoned food, equipment and supplies.

For two days, the Buffalo Soldiers suffered. Before they reached Double Lakes, wrote an officer later, "the crazed survivors of our men" were "fighting each his neighbor for the blood of the horses as the animals' throats were cut." We had "madmen" on our hands. The soldiers survived by drinking their urine and the urine of their horses, by sucking on the moist internal organs of their dead mounts and by their grim determination to struggle forward.

The first soldiers stumbled into Double Lakes about 4:00 a.m. on July 30. They refreshed themselves and headed back to help others who remained on the trail. Two weeks later, most of the men were back at Fort Concho.

The expedition captured national attention: "The Staked Plains Horror," newspapers called it at the time. Four men died, many deserted, one went mad, leadership failed and the whole company broke up. Bad luck, missed opportunities, unusually hot weather and ill-fated decisions all played a hand in the July 1877 tragedy.

Part 10

BEAVER, BISON, BONES AND BEEF

On the heels of the explorers of the Llano Estacado came the hunters. Long before bison hunters invaded the region, trappers came in 1832 seeking beaver. Although they found none, their record of the trip provides a valuable insight into Comanche life on the Llano.

Forty years later, bison hides had become a valuable commodity. Hunters soon invaded the region from the north and south, in spite of promises made to Comanche and Kiowa leaders that the area was for their exclusive use. They soon retaliated at Adobe Walls and Yellow House Canyon, but they could not stop the invasion of hundreds of hunters who virtually exterminated the southern bison herd within five years. Soon, millions of bison were replaced by thousands of cattle brought to the region by pioneer ranchers.

But left behind on the prairies were tons of bison bones, which for many struggling pioneer farmers became a source of income in desperate times.

15

Down Blackwater Draw in 1832

Paul H. Carlson

In 1832, at the height of the great Mountain Man beaver-trapping era in the Rocky Mountains, some forty-five trappers from Taos and Santa Fe headed down Blackwater Draw in search of beaver grounds in the upper Brazos River country and in the headstreams of nearby rivers.

They found no beaver, as it turns out, but their adventures riding down the draw through what today is Mackenzie Park, the Buffalo Springs recreation area and the lower Yellow House Canyon reveal plenty about life on the Llano Estacado in the 1830s.

Leaders of the expedition included Albert Pike, a poet, journalist, lawyer and, during the Civil War, a Confederate general; Bill Williams, usually a loner and one of the more successful Mountain Men of the West; and John Harris of Missouri, who sponsored the expedition.

Once across the Pecos River, the trappers climbed the western Caprock onto the Llano Estacado, "a place," some members of the expedition believed, "from which we could not escape alive." The "Staked Prairie," as Pike called it, gave off "the appearance always of having been scorched by fire." The buffalo and grama grass of late September was brown.

They found the dry upper reaches of Blackwater Draw. As they started down the waterless stream, they discovered that even as early as 1832 the draw contained well-worn paths across the Llano. The "road" they followed, wrote Pike, "was now broad and plain, consisting of 14 or 15 horse trails side by side." Obviously, Native Americans, comancheros and others had been using the draw for several decades, at least since the 1780s, when comancheros began annual trading expeditions to the Southern Plains.

Pike and the trappers found "plenty of sign of wild horses." When seeking water, they sometimes entered the sand hills (the Muleshoe Dunes along Blackwater Draw) and hunted there.

The trappers also discovered that life was not always easy on the Llano. They were constantly short of water. Because wild game for food was scarce or difficult to catch, they were always hungry. The men found and killed a bison on a couple of occasions, but deer, antelope and other game frequently escaped them. They ate horse flesh but often had little fire with which to cook it, as there was not much wood for fuel. A few times, they burned the ordure of horses. Other times, they "could only make a blaze of tall weeds."

In addition, members of the expedition found that some Comanches also went hungry. While riding down Blackwater Draw, they encountered three separate Comanche camps, or rancherias. The first one, located in the draw but near the sand hills and perhaps in modern Lamb County, contained twenty lodges. The people were "extremely poor," Pike noted. "They had no blankets—no buffalo robes—no meat—and were dressed shabbily." Their lodges were old and warn, but they had a herd of one thousand horses and mules.

The second one, located somewhere near present-day Mackenzie Park or perhaps at Buffalo Springs, may have been in better condition. Most of the Comanche men were absent, hunting, and "as we approached," wrote Pike, "the women mounted their horses and took to the hills." Still, the beaver trappers were able to trade for some meat and nuts.

The third Comanche camp was located about thirty-five miles downstream from the second. The valley was wider here and it "was full of small hills interspersed with [mesquite] bushes." Pike counted fifty lodges, "much handsomer" than those in the other villages, and lots of horses. As with the other camps, no warriors were present. The men were hunting or engaged in some kind of fight with either American or New Mexican traders. Apparently, a major confrontation had occurred in which dozens of wagons had been destroyed. Possibly, they had fought with a caravan of comancheros with their two-wheeled carts.

As women in all three Comanche camps had cut and mangled their legs in mourning for lost loved ones, warriors had died. Pike thought it was during "the attack on the wagons."

The trappers followed down Yellow House Canyon before turning north. They did not find the beaver they were looking for, and the expedition

Albert Pike and his party may have traversed this part of the North Fork of the Double Mountain Fork of the Brazos River southeast of present-day Lubbock. *Courtesy Ellen Carlson.*

broke up. Pike, with some men, headed for Arkansas; others, led by Bill Williams, returned to Santa Fe by a northern route, perhaps along the Canadian River Valley.

A couple of things about the expedition warrant emphasis. First, one should note that several reports, such as Pike's, indicate as early as 1832 that some Comanches, although owning large horse herds, were otherwise destitute, suffering from food shortages and poor housing. And, second, Blackwater and Yellow House draws in 1832 were already busy. For at least forty years, comancheros coming from New Mexico had been using the normally well-watered routes to reach trading sites in Casas Amarillas, Ransom Canyon, Muchaque Peak, Silver Falls and elsewhere in Comanche country.

16
BISON HUNTERS

PAUL H. CARLSON

Bison hunters are often depicted as tough, destructive and nasty characters who nearly did to the big majestic animals what others did to passenger pigeons and dodo birds.

Richard Irving Dodge, a military officer who knew them, said bison hunters were a rough and smelly bunch, as "unsavory as a skunk." One of them, Jim McIntire, bragged that he had "killed Comanche and Kiowa Indians by the score, and once I killed and skinned [an Indian woman] and made a purse of her breast."

Indians resented the assault hunters made on bison herds, and by the 1920s, forty years after the fact, "magazine and newspaper articles" had begun to "claim the killing of the buffalo [was] a national calamity."

It was a tragedy, most would agree. And perhaps bison hunters were disgusting. But J. Wright Mooar, one of the most successful bison hide men in Texas, disagreed. "I resent [such] ignorance," he said in 1928. "The killing of the buffalo [was not] accomplished by vandals." Indeed, he said, "Buffalo hunting was a business and not a sport; it required capital, management and work, lots of work, more work than anything else." Sometimes it was dangerous. Men might get caught in stampedes. Wolves were always present.

And, in Texas, Comanches and Kiowas resented the presence of hide men in territory that they understood the federal government, without consent from the State of Texas, had set aside as their hunting preserve.

The big bison slaughter began in the 1870s in Kansas. Hunters quickly reduced the herds there and in eastern Colorado. Then, some hunters went north toward the Montana Plains. Many others rode south. They entered the Texas Panhandle about 1873 and the Rolling Plains country around Fort Griffin soon afterward.

In late 1876, some hunters, led by Charles Rath, headed south from the Panhandle to get below the herds in the upper Brazos and Colorado rivers region. From towns in Shackelford and Stonewall counties, the bison hunters spread west and south. Leading hunters included Mooar and his brother John Wesley Mooar, John R. Cook, George Causey, Bill Benson and the well-to-do English former seamen brothers James H. and Robert Cator.

Hunting parties usually went out in teams: a hunter with a powerful rifle (a popular type was called a "Big Fifty"); a couple of hide skinners, a teamster; and perhaps a camp orderly who cooked, spread hides to dry near the camp and watched the area.

The hunter searched for a spot on the edge of a herd where he could get a "stand," as it was called. At that place, he would shoot an animal, usually a bull—their hides brought greater return. Then, usually, he would kill any bison—bull or cow—that became restless or seemed about to leave and draw the herd away. In such fashion, the hunter might kill a very large number of animals. In 1877, a surveyor heading west found in Archer County "a country marked by a great number of glistening skeletons of buffaloes, apparently slaughtered one or two years earlier." The bones, he wrote, covered two "spots of ten acres each" with an estimated one hundred "skeletons closely lying, as the result of a hunter getting what was called a 'stand.'"

Then the skinners moved in. A "capable man," wrote E. Douglas Branch, "could skin fifty buffaloes a day." Sometimes skinners got paid by

A bison hunter camp. *Courtesy Southwest Collection, Texas Tech University, Lubbock, Texas.*

the hide (twenty-five to thirty cents each), but the "usual pay was about fifty dollars a month."

Bigger outfits often used horses. In this method, wrote Branch, a skinner cut the hide from head to tail and "loosened the hide from the legs, the head, and the tail." Then, ropes were fastened from the hide to a horse, "and the tugs of the horse pulled the hide from the flesh." Men carried the hides to camp and pegged them on the ground. Branch indicated that "strips of flesh that adhered [to the hide] were scraped off, and the hide left to dry."

The teamster, while others continued hunting and skinning, hauled the dried hides to Rath City in Stonewall County or to Fort Griffin and returned with supplies, including food, whiskey, lead, gunpowder, shells and other necessities. In such fashion, the hunt in Texas went on through most months each year. At the peak of the hunt, in 1877–78, perhaps four thousand men (hunters, skinners, teamsters and buyers) sought hides in West Texas.

In the two-month period from December 1877 through January 1878, Charles Rath and his partners purchased perhaps two hundred thousand hides at Rath City. They paid about two dollars for a good bull hide and a bit less for a female one.

During the three and a half years that the little town existed, an estimated 1.1 million hides passed through it. At the end of 1879, Rath City was a ghost town and the bison hunt in Texas was mostly over.

17

THE RATH TRAIL

Paul H. Carlson

Charles Rath, a merchant, entrepreneur and bison hunter, opened the Rath Trail in 1876. In Texas, it stretched from Mobeetie and old Fort Elliott in Wheeler County south to Rath City (now gone) in Stonewall County, or about eight miles north of modern Hamlin.

Essentially, it followed present-day U.S. Highway 83, the "Main Street of the Great Plains." It ran through Wheeler, Collingsworth, Childress, Cottle, King and Stonewall counties.

Rath laid out the road as a way to get bison hunters and their followers south of the large bison herds still roaming West Texas. And he opened the road to ease the problem of moving hunter supplies and equipment south to his trade center and hides north to market in Dodge City, Kansas.

Until late 1877, Dodge City was the main hide market. There, Rath and his partners operated a large trading store and mercantile, and they handled hundreds of thousands of bison hides. To further the trade, Rath and his partners were among the first merchants to build a store near Adobe Walls on the north banks of the Canadian River in the Panhandle, a former and, in 1874, a current trading site, as well as a place where, in the same year, Comanches, Kiowas and Cheyennes attacked in an effort to drive the merchants and bison hunters away.

The Indian warriors enjoyed mixed success. They did not overrun Adobe Walls, but the merchants, teamsters, hunters and skinners (perhaps twenty-eight in all, including one woman) who survived the attack left temporarily

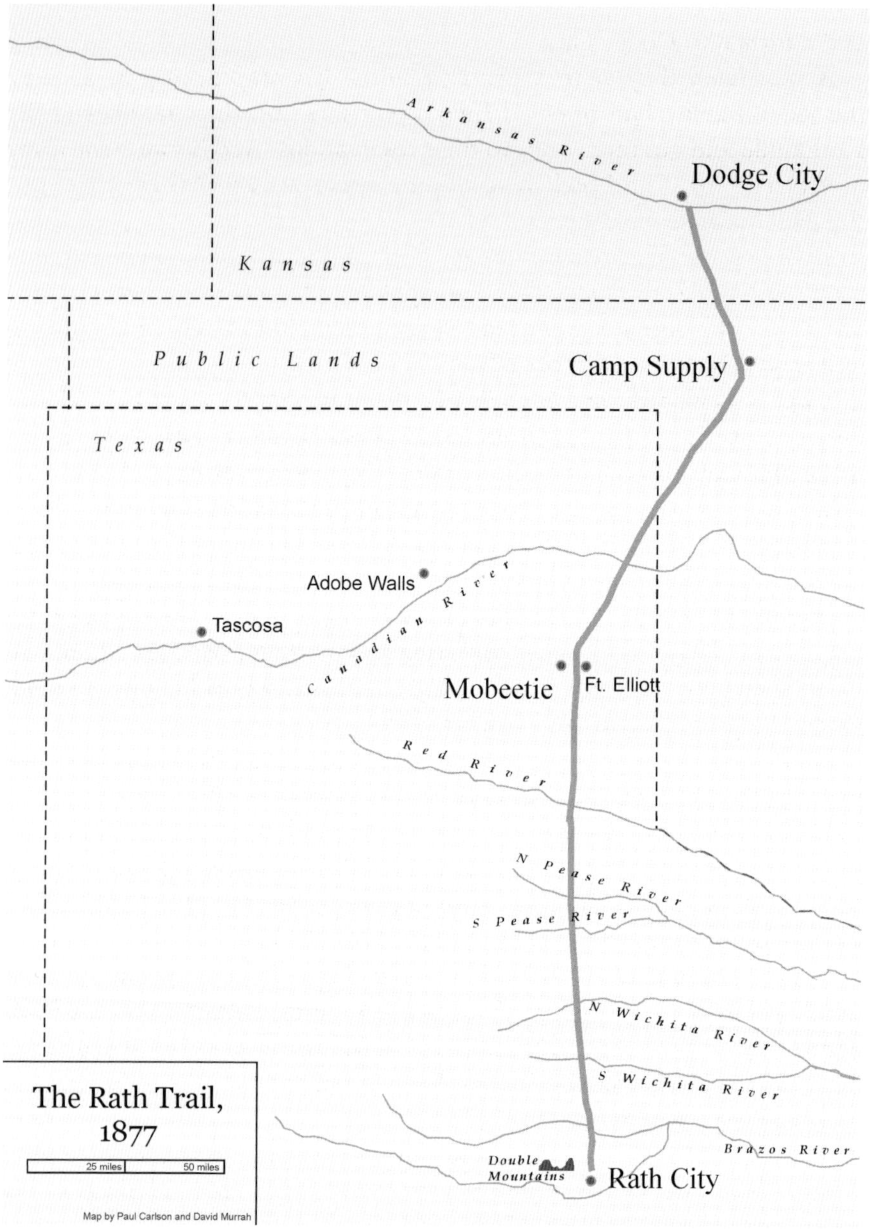

The Rath Trail ran from Dodge City, Kansas, to Rath City, the short-lived trading community in Stonewall County. *Map by Paul Carlson and David Murrah.*

and returned to Dodge City.

A year later, they were back. This time, they stayed, in part because the federal army had pursued Indian warriors and their families in the Panhandle and got them back to their reservations. And because the army in February 1875 had built Fort Elliott in what became Wheeler County, the Panhandle seemed safe.

To supply the increasing number of bison hunters, a well-worn wagon road ran south from Dodge City through Camp Supply to Mobeetie, a little community for supplying hunters, sheepherders and traders in the area as well as soldiers at nearby Fort Elliott.

Some writers, including Ida Ellen Rath, argue that the route from Dodge City is properly called the "Rath Trail." Perhaps she is correct, for it was in Dodge City that Charles Rath talked his partner Robert Wright into risking a large part of the firm's capital in the venture. There also Rath convinced W.M.D. Lee of the large Lee & Reynolds trading firm—the "Big Contractors," they were called—to go in with Wright and him. Rath was in charge of the operation. He and John Russell, wagon master of the Rath freight train, acquired wagons and oxen to pull them, building equipment for the new town and supplies for hunters, including merchandise, whiskey, tobacco, foodstuffs, guns and ammunition.

As Russell began loading operations, bison hunters got their outfits together. According to Ms. Rath, there "were perhaps fifty wagons in all in the train." They made it to Fort Elliott without difficulty.

At Fort Elliott, Lee & Reynolds assembled their supplies and added a large number of wagons to the train. The traders got laundryman Charlie Sing with his equipment, some scouts and perhaps others to join the caravan. J. Wright Mooar, one of the bison hunters, said that "there were two or three hundred wagons in the outfit." The number seems too large, but Ms. Rath argues that with freight wagons from the two firms, wagons belonging to the hunters who had left Dodge City and others "who joined along the way, the number does not seem out of line."

Thus, in the fall of 1876, loaded and organized, the huge procession started. Forty-year-old Rath, sitting on horseback with a compass in his hand, led the way from Fort Elliott heading due south.

Behind Rath in the first wagon rode Russell and twelve road builders. Using picks, shovels, axes and other road-building equipment, they chopped trees and shrubs, removed large rocks and graded passable roadways down creek- and riverbanks and through draws and arroyos along the route. They moved south in as straight a line as possible. Following the first wagon, company

Charles Rath, promoter of Rath City, sits on a large pile of bison hides hauled to Dodge City, Kansas, circa 1877. *Courtesy Southwest Collection, Texas Tech University.*

teamsters and bullwhackers moved tons of equipment and supplies. Bison hunters, skinners, saloon operators, traders, storekeepers and others moved their wagons into the long line. One wagon, or so the story goes, carried several women who planned to operate a dance hall.

In December 1876, after several weeks on the trail, Rath led the procession onto a stretch of level ground above the Double Mountain Fork of the Brazos River in Stonewall County. There, not far from the Double Mountains, he laid out the short-lived town of Rath City.

During the next two years, Rath's teamsters carried supplies to his namesake town and hauled away tens of thousands of hides, following the compass-straight road he had charted on horseback.

18

THE CATTLE KINGDOM ON THE LLANO ESTACADO

DAVID J. MURRAH

By 1878, the great buffalo slaughter on the Southern Plains had ended, and government officials had moved Comanche and Kiowa people to reservations in the Indian Territory (modern-day Oklahoma).

With the nearest railroad more than three hundred miles away, one last barrier—isolation—remained in the way of the settlement on the great open plains and prairies of the Llano Estacado. But, for those willing to take large risks, the splendid grasses of the Llano became available. In fact, for several years, sheepherders from New Mexico had summered their flocks along the breaks of the Canadian River and even into the shallow valleys of Running Water Draw and Yellow House Canyon.

The first cattleman was Charles Goodnight. In 1876, he moved a large herd from Colorado and across the northwestern Llano to Palo Duro Canyon. The following year, C.C. Slaughter moved herds from South Texas into the canyons below the southern escarpment near present-day Lamesa.

Other cattlemen soon followed. In 1878, Hank Smith of Fort Griffin obtained control of some six hundred head of cattle located along the headwaters of White River, in Blanco Canyon, north of present-day Crosbyton. There, Smith moved his family in November 1878 to a large rock house, constructed the previous year in the canyon. In so doing, the Smiths became the first permanent settlers in the Llano Estacado area.

Smith's descriptions of rich pasture and abundant water attracted the attention of free-grass ranchers who quickly filled the region east of the

Charles Goodnight (*left*) and C.C. Slaughter pioneered cattle ranching on the Llano Estacado. The two grew up in Palo Pinto County, Texas, and served together in the military during the Civil War. *Goodnight photo public domain; Slaughter photo courtesy George M. Slaughter family.*

Llano Estacado escarpment. By 1880, there were thousands of cattle grazing along the scattered streams, but less than two hundred people occupied the vast area, and nearly half of those comprised the Quaker community of Estacado in northeastern Lubbock County.

The first cattlemen used an open, unfenced range, claiming grazing rights on extensive tracts simply by placing their cattle on the land and by controlling access to the limited water resources.

But the open-range, free-grass era did not last. As eastern and European investors learned of the high profits being made, they rushed into West Texas, purchased range rights or outright title to land and fenced the property, thereby squeezing out smaller operations. The large operators used new technology to their advantage, namely barbed wire, windmills and railroads.

By 1884, many of the large open-range ranches were enclosed, and men controlling the land were poised to solidify their cattle kingdom. With cheap grass, freedom from Indian raids, little taxation, favorable weather conditions and constantly rising prices, most prospered.

Weather soon changed good fortune. On January 16, 1885, a howling blizzard marked the beginning of the end of the cattle kingdom. The storm killed thousands of cattle. Then, in the following summer, a two-year drought began, only to be followed by another devastating snowstorm in January 1887. That storm drove cattle from the Plains all the way to the Pecos River.

The disastrous weather, combined with an unprecedented price collapse, ruined many cattlemen, both big and small. And, in time, the same technologies that had built the cattle kingdom—windmills, barbed wire and railroads—hastened its demise.

Once railroads penetrated the heart of the Llano Estacado (especially after 1907), land values skyrocketed, and the few big ranchers remaining sold out to hundreds of small farmer-stockmen. But remnants of some ranches survived. The oldest and most historic ranch of the Llano Estacado, the JA, established in 1876 by Charles Goodnight and John Adair, remains in operation in Palo Duro Canyon along the headwaters of the Red River.

Another survivor was the operation of C.C. Slaughter. After the open-range era, he acquired blocks of land in Lynn, Cochran, Hockley, Hale and Lamb counties and invested heavily in windmills to provide water. At the peak of his operation in 1905, he owned or controlled nearly one million acres and forty thousand cattle.

One of the most unique and most successful of the early ranches was the Matador Land and Cattle Company. First established in 1879 by H.H. Campbell on open range in Motley, Cottle, Floyd and Dickens counties, the Matador Ranch was purchased by Scotland investors in 1882. It operated until 1951.

While most of the surviving ranches were located primarily below the Caprock, a few remained on the windswept Plains. At Double Lakes in northwestern Lynn County, Cass O. Edwards in 1883 located his T-Bar Ranch, which became one of the largest ranches situated entirely above the Caprock. The T- Bar continues to operate in western Lynn County. Similarly, in Hockley County, remnants of the Spade and Mallet ranches, established in 1889 and 1895, respectively, are still used for ranching.

Ironically, the number of cattle grazing on the Llano Estacado in the 1880s during the heyday of the Cattle Kingdom is only a fraction of the total bovines present there today.

Through the development of feedlots utilizing corn and other feed grains raised on surrounding farms, ranchers and farmer-stockmen have found a way to make the region one of the greatest producers of fed cattle in the world.

19

Picking Bison Bones for Profit

John T. "Jack" Becker

Two lines from the song "Homesteaders Ballad" sum up the early life of some of the first settlers on the Great Plains. They are: "We pick up bones to keep from starving, / And we picked up chips to keep from freezing."

The words to the song probably came closer to reflecting the truth than romanticizing the past when sung by early Llano Estacado settlers who lived through hard times before Lubbock and surrounding counties became "settled up."

All through the 1880s and 1890s, the earliest settlers of the area could depend on bison bone picking for a source of income. If crops failed and cattle died, one dependable source of income was the bone trade.

A successful bone trade depended on three factors: a ready source of bones (supply), manufacturers who had need for the bones (demand) and transportation to get the bones from West Texas to eastern markets (railroads). In the years before the turn of the last century, all three factors occurred, producing a profitable—although temporary—industry at just the right time for early Lubbock and surrounding county pioneers.

The great kill-off of bison during the 1870s left millions of buffalo bones strewn across the prairies of West Texas, undisturbed for fifteen or more years. A boom period of bone picking followed. Eastern industrialists found a use for animal bones in the manufacture of fertilizer, sugar, china, buttons and handles. And railroads made it possible for the supply of bison bones to reach manufacturers, which made the trade possible.

This stack of bison skulls and bones at an unknown place in the late 1800s illustrates the vast quantity of bones gathered for shipment. *Public domain.*

In slack times, when duties around the farm or ranch eased up, early settlers gathered bones for sale. It was a job even children could do. A farm wagon with sideboards attached could haul between four and five tons of bones. Two men or a man and his family could pick up that many bones in a single day. If the bones were scattered thickly on the ground, a picker could gather half a ton of bones without moving the wagon. Picking bones was the easy part.

Freighting the bones to distant railheads, called boneheads, took the most time and of course was expensive. In the early days, the nearest boneheads to Lubbock were Abilene, Colorado City and Amarillo.

But if crops failed or many cattle died, bone picking was the only thing that kept people from going hungry. In the late 1870s, bones brought from four to six dollars per ton. Through the years, the price of bones rose as the demand for them increased and the bones became harder to find. By the late 1890s, bone pickers received between twenty and twenty-two dollars a ton.

Many early Lubbock freighters learned that they could make money hauling bones to Amarillo or Colorado City and then freight much-needed supplies back to Lubbock. Oscar and Rob Tubbs, sons of early Lubbock pioneer Isham Tubbs, remembered helping their father gather bison bones and hauling them to Colorado City in the 1890s. There, they sold them to a bone dealer for twenty dollars a ton. After a deal for the bones was made, the freighter weighed his wagonload of bones and then piled them in a long row beside the railroad track.

The piles of bones reached unimaginable sizes. In 1881, a pile of bones in Abilene measured thirty feet wide at the base, reached the height of a one-story building and ran four blocks long. That year in July, August and September, 109 railcars left Abilene headed east loaded with 1,635 tons of bison bones. In 1888, a pile of bones at Colorado City reached ten feet high, thirty feet wide at the base, and extended nearly a half mile in length.

After 1890, cattle bones began slowly to replace bison bones. After several bad years of droughts, blizzards, inadequate care and predatory animals, bone pickers found large quantities of cattle bones often at places called "die ups." Cattle bones did not bring as high a price as bison skeletons, mainly because they were not as heavy as bison. They brought about eight dollars a ton.

Some writers have estimated that during the boom years—the 1880s and 1890s—of the bone trade, railroads shipped half a million tons of bison bones out of West Texas, which put $3 million into the pockets of early pioneers.

The bison bone trade and, to a lesser extent, the cattle bone business, made an important contribution to the livelihood of early pioneers, stimulated the freighting industry and supported railroads as the big trains entered West Texas.

Part V

TEXAS'S LAST FRONTIER

In 1890, had you decided to travel due west from the tiny village of Lubbock, you would not have encountered a farmstead or community until you struck the Pecos and Roswell, New Mexico, 166 miles to the west.

Your route would have passed through the heart of the Llano Estacado—a waterless stretch of prairie framed by sand hills, the most isolated of all the region. It became the last land on the Llano to be claimed and occupied.

This chapter focuses on surveyors and those entrepreneurial pioneers who brought closure to what some have called Texas's last frontier. It includes accounts of legendary cattlemen Charles Goodnight, David M. DeVitt and C.C. Slaughter.

20

Surveyors in Lubbock County in 1877

Paul H. Carlson

In 1876, the Texas state legislature in a single act created fifty-four counties in West Texas, carving them out of the huge Bexar Land District. Lubbock County, named for Civil War hero and former Texas Ranger Thomas Saltus Lubbock, was one of them.

In response to the legislative act, speculators, real estate companies and surveyors moved into the new but unorganized counties to locate lands in the public domain and sell them to people from Kentucky, Illinois, Missouri and elsewhere. One of the surveying companies was a Dallas firm known as Daugherty, Connelle and Ammerman. In the spring of 1877, the firm sent out two parties of surveyors. One unit went west through Fort Worth, Granbury and Stephenville to Eastland (the firm's frontier headquarters), where it met the firm's other group.

From the busy little town, Robert Ammerman led six men from the firm to the northwest corner of Archer County and from there planned to survey west to the New Mexico border.

Plans changed. On July 7, several miles east of Roaring Springs, the surveyors caught sight of the Llano Estacado in the distance. One of them remembered, "Standing out against the western sky there was an immense barricade level with the sky, stretching north and south and marked by recesses, parapets and peneplain like a Middle Age fortification."

On July 13, they were in Blanco Canyon at the old Dewey's Lake north of Silver Falls in Crosby County. "The lake was very small," one of them wrote,

One survey party camped at the site of Hank Smith's rock house in Blanco Canyon while it was still under construction in 1877. *Courtesy Southwest Collection, Texas Tech University.*

"and seemed to be the remnant of an old beaver dam." The next day, they came to Hank and Elizabeth Smith's unfinished "Rock House." Here, near Ranald Mackenzie's 1873 military trail, they camped for a day with Rock House stonemasons and with a family of four from Erath County on its way to New Mexico.

On August 1, the surveyors were in Lubbock County. They reached Blackwater Draw, which they called "the North Fork of the Yellowhouse Creek," somewhere near present-day Lubbock Country Club. At nightfall, they arrived at "some springs around which were a great number of buffaloes and antelopes." They found evidence of a recently abandoned Indian camp, including lodge poles and an old saddle of Indian design.

The next day, the surveyors crossed over to what they called "the West Fork of Yellowhouse Creek," present-day Yellow House Draw. About a mile south of the creek they saw a herd of one thousand or more bison stretched out before them. They quietly watched the animals for a time—it was the height of mating season—when suddenly the herd stampeded away.

The surveyors moved down the Yellow House and passed its junction with Blackwater Draw in present Mackenzie Park. Below the junction, they reported, the stream was three feet deep and five feet wide. In places it was "choked with skeletons of buffaloes...[and] a great abundance of small catfish" were present.

About noon on August 3, Indians, they thought, were attacking. One of the surveyors, O.W. Williams, wrote, "We promptly unhitched our animals, got out arms and cartridges, and under our wagon lined our guns on the spokes of the wheels ready for good shooting."

The Indians proved to be bison hunters who had been part of the tragic soldier-hunter expedition chasing after Comanches on the western Llano Estacado. Under an unrelenting hot sun, expedition members ran out of water, got lost and suffered desperately. The soldiers and hunters left behind supplies, food and equipment. They drank their own urine. When a horse died, they cut open the animal's belly to suck on the wet internal organs of their mounts. Four soldiers died. The expedition broke up and separated.

Now, probably near Buffalo Springs, the surveyors fed the hunters who had found water at the present-day Lubbock Lake Site. The next day, August 4, the hunters left for Muchaque Peak and Bull Creek in Borden County, where they had a cache of supplies. The surveyors continued down Yellow House Creek and passed present-day Ransom Canyon before heading toward the Smith property in Blanco Canyon. After camping a day below the Rock House, they turned east toward home.

In Lubbock County in 1877, the surveyors marked off available land sites. They saw bison, deer, antelope and turkeys. They reported seeing only shinnery oak and tiny mesquite trees.

They found water in the principal streams and on the level Plains plenty of grass. But, as a result of a two-month drought, the grass was dry and brown, giving off an impression that much of Lubbock County in 1877 looked like a never-ending desert.

21

Texas's Last Frontier

David J. Murrah

The Llano Estacado stretches from Hobbs, New Mexico, on the southwest to Pampa, Texas, on the northeast, and from north of Clovis, New Mexico, on the northwest, to just south of Midland.

The heart of the Llano Estacado—and historically the most isolated part of the region—is a thirty-mile-wide swath that stretches westward from Lubbock about one hundred miles to the western escarpment of the Llano in eastern New Mexico.

This is a most intriguing area, made so by its lack of surface water and settlers. Along its border on the north and south there were some limited water sources. On the north side was the Punta de Agua, near present-day Lubbock. From there, Yellow House Draw snaked to the northwest before giving way to being just a remnant of an ancient riverbed. A string of "lost" lakes—Silver Lake, Bull Lake, Illusion Lake and Coyote Lake—provided the only water for man and animals, and often it was saline.

About thirty miles to the south lay another string of natural lakes in Lynn and Terry counties, the most prominent being Tahoka Lake, Mound Lake and Rich Lake. Then, to the west of the string of lakes on both the north and south ends of the heart of the Llano, one encounters even more intriguing natural boundaries—ranges of sand dunes. On the north side are the Muleshoe Sand Hills, the largest contiguous section of sand to be found on the Llano. They extend more than one hundred miles from west to

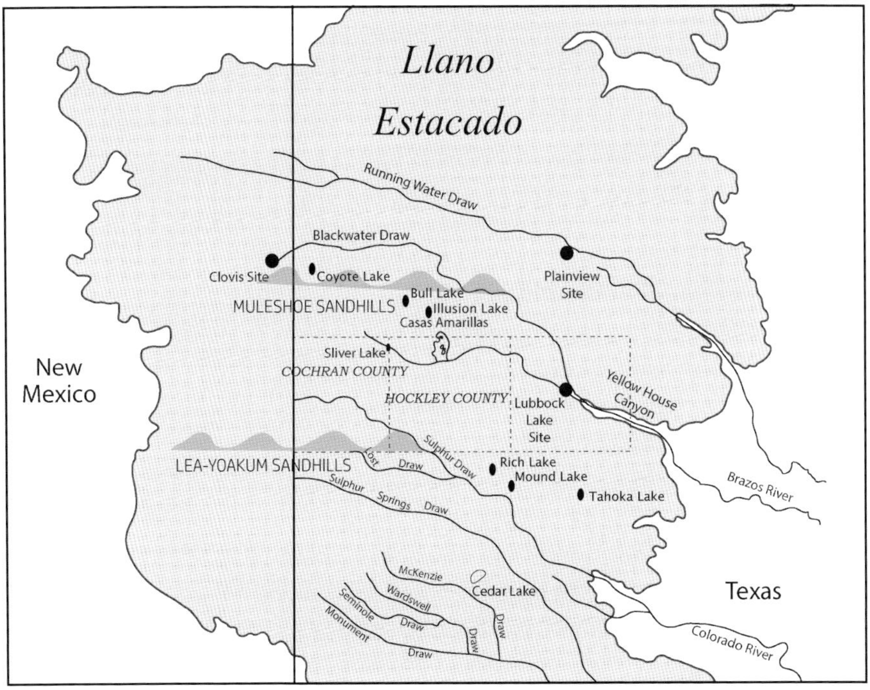

Cochran and Hockley counties were among the state's last to be settled. The area became known as Texas's last frontier. *Base map by Curtis Peoples, enhanced by David Murrah.*

east from western Roosevelt County to the western edge of Hale County in Texas and range in width from ten to two miles.

A slightly smaller but similar range of sand hills borders the region on the south side. These are the Lea-Yoakum Dunes, sometimes called the Mescalero Dunes, that begin at the western escarpment of the Llano Estacado in northern Lea County, New Mexico, and extend east-southeast along the Cochran and Yoakum County line and into Terry County.

Between the two ranges of sand hills, there are no natural water sources and few playa lakes. The only break in the otherwise level expanse is the shallow Sulphur Draw, which heads in west-central Cochran County near present-day Bledsoe and meanders to the southeast to merge with Lost Draw in central Terry County at present-day Brownfield.

During wet seasons, a few scattered springs along Sulphur Draw once represented the only freshwater available. The flanking sand hills were discouraging barriers. Supposedly, even the earliest of the region's occupants, the Plains Indians, avoided the mysterious dunes. Their legends told how a devastating storm had filled with sand what once had been a beautiful river and paradise, leaving only the drifting sand dunes on the Llano Estacado.

However, springs along Sulphur Draw and at Silver Lake actually flowed for hundreds of years, providing paleo-era hunters with water and game—now-extinct mammoth, bison, camels and horses—which gathered at the isolated springs.

Hundreds of years later, Comanches used the isolated sand hills both as a route from the eastern Llano and as a place of refuge. If water could be found, the area offered an abundance of game, including, bison, pronghorn antelope, deer and prairie chickens. For example, Albert Pike's famous encounter with the Llano Estacado in 1832 found a large Comanche camp in the vicinity of the Muleshoe Sand Hills in present-day Lamb or Hockley County.

By the late 1870s, the Comanches were gone, along with the vast bison herds that once roamed the area. With these barriers removed, the Llano Estacado seemed ready for settlement. In 1881, the Texas & Pacific Railway built west from Fort Worth to El Paso, creating emerging trade centers at Abilene, Sweetwater, Colorado City and Midland. By 1887, the Fort Worth & Denver had reached the site of Amarillo and was pushing on to the northwest.

But not many settlers arrived. In 1890, the time at which Frederick Jackson Turner has famously claimed that the American frontier had ended, the entire Llano Estacado had only eight thousand residents, and most of those lived along the eastern escarpment of the Plains. And in what is now Cochran, Hockley, Bailey and Lamb counties—a region sixty miles square—there were only four occupants. These were probably cowboys at the Yellow House division of the large XIT Ranch.

Not until well into the twentieth century did the first plows turn sod in the region. In fact, Cochran and Hockley counties were among the last in the state to be settled, and the region rightfully earned its moniker, "Texas's Last Frontier."

22

Closing Texas's Last Frontier

David J. Murrah

Folks in Cochran and Hockley counties call their region Texas's last frontier. Indeed, it once was a virtually waterless, isolated region flanked by sand hills on the north and south.

Settlement came slowly to the area. Neither county had enough settlers to justify organization of county government until 1921 for Hockley and 1924 for Cochran. But the delay had more to do with Texas land policy than isolation. After the state ceded its claim to portions of New Mexico and Colorado in 1850, it still had ninety-eight million acres of public domain. By the early 1880s, much of this was deeded to railroads in exchange for rail lines. Nearly all of the railroad land was surveyed in sections, with the alternate sections retained by the state to sell to benefit public school funds. Big ranches would acquire the railroad land and would either lease the state-owned land or use it for free if there was no demand.

But the railroads passed over most of the western Llano due to its isolation. Thus, when the state decided in 1879 to build its present state capitol in exchange for land, it had only five million acres of the isolated prairies of the western Panhandle and South Plains to offer. From this block, the Capitol Syndicate, the developers of the XIT Ranch, chose three million acres, including the northern portion of Hockley County, leaving only about 1.2 million acres of unassigned lands in the Panhandle-Plains area. Most of this land lay in Hockley, Cochran and Bailey counties.

When the Texas legislature met in 1881, it realized that much of the public domain was gone, and yet it had not set aside land to provide school funds for the yet to be organized counties in Texas. Thus, the legislature designated three hundred leagues, or 1.2 million acres, for the unorganized counties, most of which lay in nearly all of Cochran and large parts of Bailey counties. This land went to fifty separate counties in 17,712 acre-blocks, or four leagues, and several more acquired smaller blocks. Each county was to hold its four-league block of land until it needed to sell it to support its public schools.

In the other parts of the region, settlers could file on 640 acres of public land and establish a homestead, often in the middle of a rancher's pasture. But in Cochran and Hockley counties, the pastures were vast and indivisible, generally two and a half miles wide and ten miles long. There, ranchers would eventually be able to lease or even buy the entirety of the large pastures. In essence, on the western Llano, the future belonged to those who could afford to control large acreage, effectively shutting out the farmer's frontier for the next forty years.

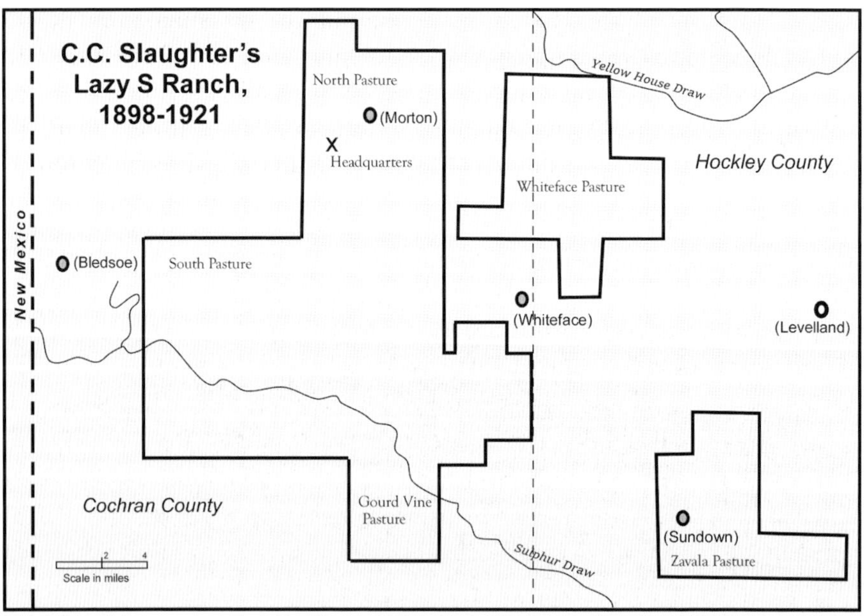

C.C. Slaughter's Lazy S Ranch was one of the last major ranches to be created from public land and encompassed nearly 250,000 acres. *Map by David Murrah.*

But in the 1880s, only a few ranchers even attempted to put cattle on the western Llano. In 1885, Scurry County rancher John Nunn moved one thousand cattle to pastures in Terry County and then bought 65,000 acres of the newly available land in Hockley and Lubbock counties, paying $1.50 per acre. This became the NUN Ranch, with its headquarters near Rich Lake, southeast of present-day Meadow.

Meanwhile, Fount G. Oxsheer of Colorado City moved cattle to land in central Hockley County in 1884. The following year, in partnership with his brothers-in-law, John and Nick Beal, he leased the Surratt pasture in southern Cochran County. Oxsheer was among the first to put windmills on the Llano Estacado. Although hard hit by drought in the late 1880s, the Beals and Oxsheer managed to operate a ranch on about one hundred thousand acres in Cochran and western Hockley counties until the 1890s. By that time, recurring drought and a national depression forced them to sell to pioneer Dallas cattleman and banker C.C. Slaughter in 1897.

With Oxsheer's help, Slaughter purchased nearly 250,000 acres of the various county school land pastures, most of which lay in a solid block, and invested heavily in fencing, windmills and water tanks. Known as the Lazy S, or White Face, Ranch, it was one of the last major ranches to be developed and became a showplace for purebred Hereford cattle and operation efficiency. Intending for the ranch to be a living inheritance for his wife and nine children, Slaughter retired in 1911 and died in 1919. By that time, drought, declining cattle prices and family discontent forced

When the Slaughter family divided the Lazy S ten ways in 1921, most of the cattle were sold or moved to other ranches. This herd was moved to El Paso. *Courtesy George M. Slaughter family.*

the Slaughter heirs to divide the ranch ten ways in 1921, and the Lazy S Ranch ceased to exist.

Some of the Slaughter heirs continued to operate smaller ranches, but others promoted a railroad and town building. Others elected to sell their land outright, which then led to the creation of the town of Morton, whose founder, Morton J. Smith, succeeded in getting his town named as the county seat over rivals Ligon and Lehman.

With the breakup of the Lazy S Ranch, it was only a matter of time until enough settlers were able to organize Cochran County government in 1924, which signaled the closing of Texas's last frontier.

23

The Last Great Fence Cutting War

David J. Murrah

In the early 1880s, after the invention of barbed wire, fence-cutting became a major point of conflict between Texas ranchers and farmers. After a special session of the Texas legislature in 1884, most of the issues were resolved.

However, in 1903, a dispute between two prominent ranchers in Hockley County led to a very expensive fence-cutting land war. The outcome ultimately cost the loser's heirs millions of dollars.

On one side of the conflict were Mallet Ranch owners David M. DeVitt of Fort Worth and W.H. Flato Jr. of Kansas City, who were leasing school land owned by various counties. The Mallet Ranch lay in the southwestern quadrant of Hockley County. On the other side was Colonel C.C. Slaughter of Dallas, who had begun to purchase tracts of county school land in the area in 1897 to form what later became the Lazy S Ranch, with its headquarters southwest of present-day Morton.

Because he was one of Texas's largest landowners, Slaughter used "secret" agents to acquire land for him. By 1899, they had obtained contracts to buy more than 50,000 acres of the land that the Mallet Ranch was leasing, including a 17,712-acre block of Edwards County land.

DeVitt and Flato immediately fought back, filing separate lawsuits against Slaughter for the right to buy Maverick, Kaufman and Edwards counties' school lands. In 1901, Slaughter won the disputes over the Kaufman and Zavala land, and in a letter to his son and ranch manager George, he bragged

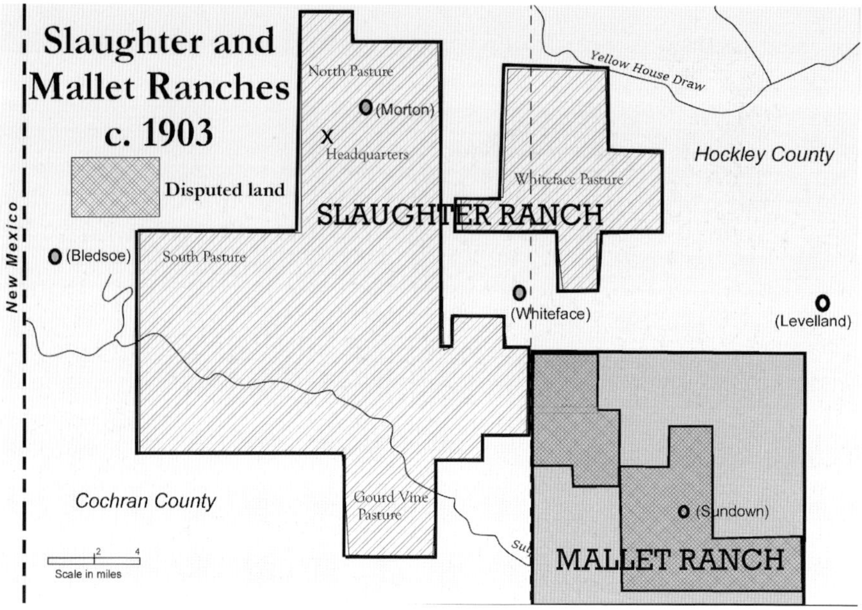

The fence-cutting war in Hockley County was the result of disputed land control between the Slaughter and Mallet ranches. *Map by David Murrah.*

that "Flato will be over here soon, wanting to compromise and telling us how much he has always loved the Slaughters."

But DeVitt and Flato were in no mood to compromise and, in 1902, exercised their right to buy the Edwards tract. When the Edwards County commissioners learned that they had violated DeVitt's lease agreement, they initially rejected both contracts but then decided to sell to DeVitt.

Slaughter ignored their decision, and when DeVitt's lease on the Edwards land expired on June 1, 1903, Slaughter's men moved onto the property and started construction of a fence. On October 19, 1903, Slaughter and DeVitt came face-to-face on the Edwards land. DeVitt said that Slaughter told him that "he had bought the land from [R.S.] Ferrell and paid his money....He said he was going to take the land and use it anyhow and that if I wanted to get any relief the [Lubbock] Court house was over there open to me."

The next day, DeVitt took Slaughter at his word and sought an injunction in the district court. Meanwhile, Slaughter's men completed the fence on October 24, 1903, but found it cut in several places later that day. Slaughter's cowboys rebuilt it—five more times—in November and December 1903.

This photo of Slaughter Ranch foreman Hiley Boyd may have been taken during the fence-cutting war in 1903, since Boyd is sporting a pearl-handled six-shooter. *Courtesy George M. Slaughter family.*

Cowboys on both sides began carrying guns, and one of Slaughter's men wore a blister from carrying a holstered gun for several weeks. Reporting the situation to his father, George Slaughter wrote, "I think he [the cowboy] thought he might be called to fight any time."

Fortunately, a leg blister was the worst casualty of the range war, but the court fight continued for two more years. On December18, 1903, Slaughter, who had some political influence, won a permanent injunction against DeVitt in a state district court. But also on that same day, DeVitt and Flato trumped Slaughter by filing papers in Missouri to incorporate as the Mallet Land and Cattle Company and to get the matter out of the state courts. On Christmas Day 1903, they filed suit in federal court against Slaughter.

The standoff on the ranches continued until late January 1904, when Slaughter, fearing a federal contempt-of-court citation, finally ordered his men to abandon their camp. On May 31, 1904, the U.S. Circuit Court ruled in favor of DeVitt and Flato, granted a permanent injunction against Slaughter and gave them title to the land.

Slaughter immediately appealed to the Court of Civil Appeals in New Orleans, but in October 1905, its judges refused to overturn the lower court's decision. The decisiveness of the appeals court's ruling apparently persuaded Slaughter to not appeal to the U.S. Supreme Court. Had Slaughter known, however, about the vast oil pool that underlay Edwards County—discovered thirty years later and named for him, the multibillion-barrel Slaughter Field—he probably would have appealed to the high court.

The Edwards County land ultimately helped make millionaires of David DeVitt's daughters, Christine DeVitt and Helen Jones. From them came two major philanthropies—the CH and Helen Jones foundations—that have contributed millions of dollars to Lubbock area hospitals, colleges and other organizations.

Part 01

MYSTERIES AND MURDER

Like the mystery of a shimmering lake on the highway ahead, which disappears before you reach it, the annals of West Texas have produced some intriguing stories of phenomena of nature, buried treasure and unsolved murders. One is that of a legendary wild white mustang that could mysteriously disappear before being captured. Other mysteries involve crimes that were solved with justice meted out, although sometimes unfairly. The story of the Hunt murders in wartime Littlefield is particularly intriguing, because justice was never completely served.

And there is the case of one of the first murder trials held on the Llano, involving legendary Lubbock attorney J.E. Vickers.

But we begin with the mystery of the Spider Rocks Maps, which has caused a number of individuals to spend decades in search of treasure.

24

Spider Rock Maps Mystery

Duane Hale

One of the greatest mysteries of West Texas is that of the so-called Spider Rocks.

The rocks, carved stone maps containing European letters of the alphabet as well as Arabic and Roman numerals, were discovered near the West Texas towns of Clyde, Aspermont and Rotan between 1902 and 1909. It was assumed that these stone maps led to buried Spanish treasure, but no treasure has been found, and the maps remain an unsolved mystery of West Texas.

The discoveries sparked unprecedented searches for gold or other treasurers in each of those areas for much of the twentieth century. Amazingly, the hundreds of people who dug holes (sometimes with bulldozers) and combed the hills of Fisher, Stonewall and Callahan counties were never able to determine who buried the treasure or what was actually buried. It was assumed that it was Spanish and that some of the symbols that were carved were numerals that appeared to be dates.

The name "Spider Rocks" comes from a spider web–like symbol on the rocks.

A sheepherder from Mexico seemed to know more than the Anglo searchers who dug up the Aspermont Rock—he was able to lead them to a Spanish sword, a silver cross and some Spanish epaulets that were buried some two hundred yards to the southwest near a ledge that was the beginning of a large ravine or canyon that ran into the Salt Fork of the Brazos River.

Also at the Aspermont site, a copper plate, a copper key and a copper dagger were found on top of the map rock.

The search began in 1902, when Dave M. Arnold arrived at the Sembritzki Ranch north of Clyde, saying that he had followed a sheepskin map that led to a buried treasure. He said that if he could find a certain map rock, he could locate the burial site.

Was Dave Arnold promoting a hoax? Anne Sembritzki Fuguay, who was a sixteen-year-old girl when the rock was dug up, stated in 1970, "My mother and father were with him when he found the map rock and they had to chop it out of the roots of a big oak tree."

One day, Arnold disappeared from Clyde and reappeared northeast of Aspermont near the forks of the Brazos River, repeating a similar story. He stayed with the Allen family, who lived along the river. Two Allen sisters, who were thirteen and fourteen years old when Arnold appeared in 1908, were interviewed in Haskell in 1971 and stated, "We believe Dave Arnold was

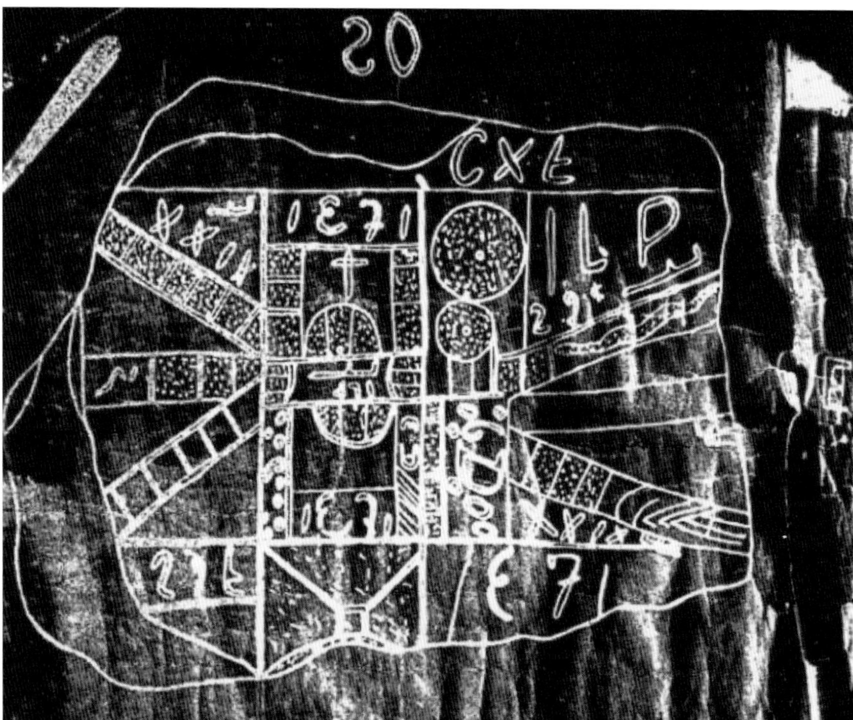

This drawing is reportedly of the inscription on the rock found by David Arnold near Clyde about 1902. *Photo from* Wichita Falls Times, *October 13, 1963. Courtesy http://www.abovetopsecret.com/forum/thread1031579/pg1.*

honest, but they plowed and plowed and they dug up the plot rock and he couldn't read a foreign thing that was on it."

Dave Arnold dug up a third Spider Rock along Gyp Creek east of Rotan in 1909. George McBeth of Rotan, a man with a good memory, was interviewed in 1976. He said, "When I was 18 years old I was hired for one day to dig for the Rotan Rock; Arnold had two groups of men digging 200 yards apart." They found a rock, and Johnny Terrell of Waco placed the Rotan Spider Rock in the Lela Lloyd Museum in Cisco, Texas.

Most of the artifacts found at Clyde and Aspermont were placed in Dr. C.L. Terrell's drugstore in Haskell and supposedly were destroyed by a fire in 1909. Terrell had financed the digging at the two sites.

Duane Hale and Steve Wilson traced down the artifacts in 1976. It seems that many of the copper plates and daggers had survived the fire, as did the epaulets, the silver cross, drawings of the Clyde Map and the Aspermont Map and letters sent in secret from the Clyde site in the year 1905. These are in the Lela Latch Lloyd Museum in Cisco. Evidently, the Aspermont and Clyde Rocks were destroyed by the fire. Joe Woods and Joe Cauble dug at Clyde as late as 1939. Cauble had also dug in Kent County near Clairemont.

Two other determined searchers were Gurney E. Ward, an Abilene photographer who was at Clyde and Aspermont from 1907 to 1911, and Frank Olmstead from LaSalle County, Illinois. Ward died in New Mexico after spending twenty-two summers digging on a site in the Sacramento Mountains that he claimed was linked to the Clyde location.

Frank Olmstead lived in a dugout northeast of Aspermont from the 1920s until his death in 1948. He was buried in one of the trenches that he had dug while searching for the Aspermont treasure.

Much knowledge of the original search at Aspermont was passed down from Bud Jones to Dock Henderson of Rule, Texas, when Jones and others returned to renew their search in 1924. Henderson was twenty-one years old and lived in a dugout on the site with Jones and his group. Henderson looked for the supposed treasure until his death in 1985.

To this day, searchers, including James and Larry Armour, continue to look for the elusive treasure of the Spider Rock Maps.

25

The Ghost of the Llano Estacado

Dan'l Richardson

Bison hunting had played out on the Llano Estacado by the end of the 1870s, and the hunters followed the last of the herds into other ranges or turned to other occupations.

One of the hunters, a Texan by way of England named Frank Collinson, took up life as a cowboy on the newly available grasslands on and around the Staked Plains. While searching for stray jinglebob cattle on top of the Caprock in 1879, Collinson came across an old buffalo hunter named Bob Payne, who told him a story about a pure white mustang he had attempted to catch for two years. The stallion, according to Payne, ranged from the Blackwater Draw up to Tierra Blanca Creek in the north. It had black eyes, the look of a Thoroughbred and was "as fleet as the wind."

The story captivated Collinson, and on a trip to Fort Sumner, New Mexico, he asked a couple of friends and noted mustangers, Pedro and Soledad Trujillo, if they had ever heard of such a horse. They told him every *mesteñero* on the plains knew about the stallion and referred to him as the "Ghost," because he vanished when anyone got too close. Many had tried to catch him.

Collinson and the Trujillo brothers agreed to partner up to catch this "Ghost." In March 1882, they met at a predetermined location on Blackwater Draw, probably in eastern Lamb County.

Collinson brought another cowboy, Dick Lane, with him, and the Trujillos had two of their own vaqueros as well as an Apache scout. By the time

The ghost of the Llano. *Sketch by H.D. Bugbee, from* My Life in the Saddle *by Frank Collinson. Used by permission of the University of Oklahoma Press.*

Collinson and Lane arrived, the Trujillos had already located the stallion and his band of about ten mares. As the horses took off toward the north at the approach of the riders, Soledad stuck a long pole in the ground with a red flag on top to mark the spot. This served as a guidepost as the hunters traded off in relays to "walk them down" in massive loops back around to their home range. The goal was to keep the horses on the move until exhaustion made them capturable.

Pedro set out after the band first, following them to the north, the Ghost "dashing over the plains, his white mane and tail blowing in the breeze." When he returned after a day, Pedro told the rest that they had gone at least twenty miles before circling to the west then turning back to the home range after dark. He estimated they had traveled at least seventy miles.

Lane took up the chase for the next leg, and on returning during the night reported the band near Spring Lake in Lamb County. The following morning, Collinson and most of the rest of the party started out after them. Collinson followed them across Running Water Draw up to Tule Draw before they turned west and began their long loop back. He camped overnight back near Blackwater Draw and resumed the chase in the morning. The mares dropped out from exhaustion, but the white stallion continued down the draw, still unbroken.

After nearing the original camp, most of the party headed south toward the Yellow Houses, and around noon on the fourth day of the chase they saw the Ghost coming west. Collinson and the unnamed Apache then followed him south toward Yellow House Lake. On reaching the bluffs overlooking the eastern edge of the alkali lake at Casas Amarillas, the stallion hesitated only a moment before plunging off into the bog twenty-five feet below. Close enough to hear the splash, Collinson reached the edge of the bluff in time to witness the last few struggles of the horse before it became engulfed in the mire, having chosen death over capture.

A reflective and slightly remorseful Collinson later said of the stallion, "He had been foaled on the best short grass that ever grew, in an invigorating climate. He had grown bigger and stronger than any other mustang I ever saw. We took after him at the time of year when range horses are at their weakest. After having been run for towards three hundred miles by successive relays of grain-fed horses, he could, at the time of his fatal jump into Yellow House Lake, have easily run away from any horse chasing him."

The mustang bands then so prevalent on the plains would soon suffer very nearly the same fate as the bison herds.

Frank Collinson's tale of the last run of the Ghost of the Llano Estacado serves as a metaphor for an important but little discussed transition in the march of time across the Texas plains. Maybe that is all it was: a story told by an old cowboy wistful for days past.

Every place needs its ghost stories, but they have a different style on the mysterious Llano Estacado.

26

Murder of James Jarrott

Chuck Lanehart

In 1900, thousands of cattle grazed vast ranches on the South Plains of Texas, but humans were few and far between. Lubbock County residents totaled less than three hundred. A few dozen ranchers occupied the unorganized counties west of Lubbock.

But changes were coming. In 1895, the Texas legislature passed the Four Sections Act, authorizing homesteaders to purchase four sections of land (2,560 acres) from the state under very favorable terms. Small entrepreneurs scurried to take advantage of the wonderful opportunity. Among them was James William Jarrott.

Jarrott was born in Alabama in 1862, but his family soon moved to Texas. In 1886, he married Mollie Wylie, a beauty from Hood County, and the couple moved to Weatherford. Representing his area, Jarrott served in the Texas House of Representatives and there won respect among his peers, developing a reputation as "fearless in speech." He met fellow legislator Charles Rogan, soon to play a pivotal role in the settlement of the Llano Estacado.

After Jarrott left the legislature, the family moved to Stephenville, where he studied law and was admitted to the bar. Although elected Erath County attorney, he was restless. Early in 1900, he traveled to Plainview to visit relatives, exploring the windswept, treeless Llano Estacado. Afterward, he heard important news from his friend Rogan, now the Texas land commissioner.

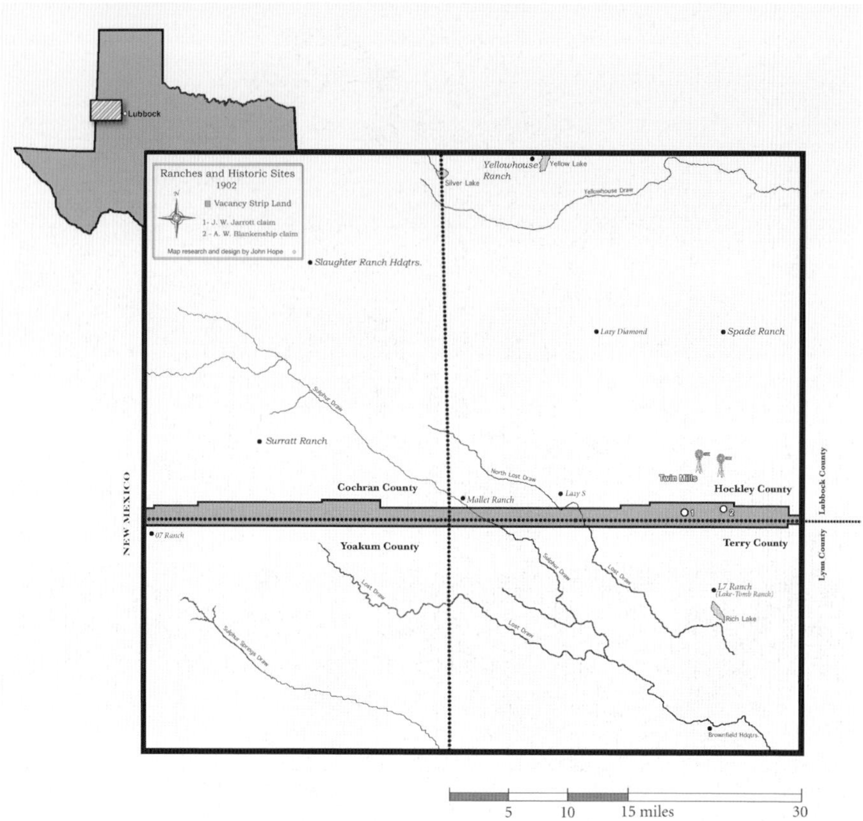

The "Jarrott Strip" was a narrow band of unclaimed land stretching west from Lubbock County for sixty miles. *Map by John Hope.*

Rogan had discovered a slice of state-owned land west of Lubbock that had not been surveyed. He intended to place the land for sale under the terms of the Four Sections Act. However, the act required the land to be surveyed. Jarrott paid for the survey, gaining an advantage over others coveting the land, soon to become known as "The Strip." The Strip extended westward sixty miles from the western boundary of Lubbock County. It crossed the south end of the unorganized counties of Hockley, Terry, Cochran and Yoakum, reaching in a narrow band to the New Mexico border.

Jarrott recruited twenty-four families from the Erath County area to join him, Mollie and their children on the arduous three-hundred-mile horse-and-wagon journey to the almost vacant South Plains. Each family claimed four sections of fertile land. It was May 1902.

James and Mollie Jarrott, circa 1900. *Courtesy Southwest Collection, Texas Tech University.*

"Deacon Jim" Miller, who reportedly shot and killed James Jarrott. *Courtesy Chuck Lanehart.*

Cattlemen already in the area did not greet the settlers warmly. Ranchers had long grazed cattle on the grassy unfenced Strip. They threatened violence, withheld precious water from windmills and filed lawsuits against the "nesters," claiming that Jarrott unfairly failed to share his survey with ranchers. Among the settlers' chief rivals were ranchers from the Lake-Tomb Cattle Company.

In far-flung courthouses scattered across the plains, Jarrott defended the settlers against the ranchers. He won all the lawsuits.

He traveled to Austin to assert the settlers' rights in the Texas General Land Office. By August, the settlers were legally established on the Strip. On August 27, Jarrott left Mollie and his children at Lubbock's Nicolett Hotel, where Mollie was recovering from an illness. The unarmed lawyer was bound for their homestead on the Strip in Hockley County. He never returned.

Someone found Jarrott's lifeless body lying in a stock tank near present-day Ropesville on land owned by the Lake-Tomb Cattle Company. He had been shot to death. Jim Jarrott was forty-one years old. It was the first documented homicide on the Texas South Plains and went unsolved for more than a century.

Those responsible for Jarrott's death thought the nesters would be scared away, but they were wrong. The settlers persisted.

Burdened with three young children, Jarrott's thirty-six-year-old widow developed the land that had cost her husband his life. She expanded the original claim to sixteen sections and raised a prime herd of cattle. Mollie married a second time, to real estate developer Monroe Abernathy. Mollie and Monroe were instrumental in bringing the railroad to Lubbock in 1909, and Mollie is considered Lubbock's first businesswoman.

Descendants of the Jarrotts, the Abernathys and other Strip settlers still reside on the South Plains.

But who killed James Jarrott? The assassin was likely "Deacon Jim" Miller, one of the most infamous gunmen of the era, responsible perhaps for fifty killings. In his recent book *Death on the Lonely Estacado: The Assassination of J.W. Jarrott, a Forgotten Hero*, author Bill Neal connects Miller to the Jarrott murder and then goes further. Neal's research clearly identifies the man who employed Miller to kill Jarrott as M.V. "Pap" Brownfield, a powerful rancher allied with the Lake-Tomb Cattle Company.

Until recently, Pap, who died in 1929, was not suspected of the crime. Ironically, the assassin's fee was likely covered by the deed to a plot of land that eventually became the City of Brownfield, named in Pap's honor.

By contrast, the man who brought the first wave of settlers to the South Plains is largely forgotten. There is no town, no school, no street named in honor of James William Jarrott. That's a shame.

27

State vs. William E. Taylor

Lubbock's First Murder Trial

Chuck Lanehart

In 1892, Lubbock citizens constructed the original county courthouse, which was located approximately in the same place as the current courthouse. The small wood-frame structure hosted little litigation until the arrival of the railroad in 1909, when Lubbock became a boomtown and was incorporated as a city. With the surge of activity, trouble followed, and the courthouse soon saw action.

Also in 1909, Lubbock elected its first mayor, Frank E. Wheelock, a founding father of Lubbock County. Wheelock took his job seriously, insisting on strict law and order, instructing a city marshal to "shoot the belly off the first man that bothers you."

Another man under Wheelock's charge was William E. Taylor, destined to be the first person tried for murder in Lubbock.

On October 24, 1912, the weekly *Lubbock Avalanche* recounted sparse details of a shooting. Feed store operator J.J. Reynolds and railroad grading contractor Tom Collins were shot dead by three pistol shots the previous Saturday evening at the Blue Front Restaurant. The city's night watchman, Taylor, was arrested at the scene and released on bail. "The *Avalanche* does not deem it wise at this time to give the particulars of the sad affair as no trial has been had to date and it would not be best to give out the particulars now," the newspaper reported. "The affair is greatly regretted by everyone, and very little is being said about it one way or another."

The Lubbock County Courthouse, circa 1912. *Courtesy Southwest Collection, Texas Tech University.*

But District Attorney J.E. Vickers knew the killings were the talk of the town. He was eager to win the first murder case to be tried in Lubbock County's new Seventy-Second District Court, created a year earlier. He quickly impaneled a grand jury. Vickers's star eyewitness, "Big Ben" Borger, told grand jurors that the victims were unarmed and were felled by Taylor because they laughed at the deputy marshal and would not be quiet. Collins bragged that he could take Taylor's gun, Borger testified.

Two murder indictments were handed down against Taylor. The Collins case was scheduled for trial first. Vickers prepared zealously, outlining compelling evidence. A miniature model of the Blue Front Restaurant—indicating locations of bodies and stray bullet holes—was constructed. Statements were reduced to typewritten memos. At least twenty-five state's witnesses were prepared to testify against Taylor.

Taylor's lawyer was William H. Bledsoe, who had arrived in Lubbock in 1908, as had Vickers. Bledsoe argued self-defense, noting: "J.J. 'Jug' Reynolds had been arrested some 10 or 12 times and had numerous fights….'Poker Tom' Collins had beaten the Negro to death….Collins hit this town on the warpath….Collins was drunk by 6 o'clock."

Twelve defense witnesses were subpoenaed, including influential names: Mayor Wheelock, Lubbock County sheriff W.H. Flynn and Coleman County sheriff W.L. Flitch. The strength of the defense case did not escape Vickers. He scrambled to overcome Bledsoe's legal obstacles.

State v. Taylor was tried in the creaky old Lubbock County Courthouse in early December 1912. Judge W.R. Spencer oversaw 108 prospective jurors and more than a week of trial proceedings.

The *Avalanche* in subtle fashion reported the verdict in the first murder trial in Lubbock's first District Court on December 13: "The trial of William E. Taylor for the killing of Thomas M. Collins in the Blue Front Restaurant in this City on the 19th day of October, which consumed last week, was given to the jury late Saturday afternoon. The jury after about three hours of deliberations, made known their desire to return a verdict, which was 'Not Guilty.'" The report continued, "This was one of the most interesting cases which has been tried in Lubbock in many days and the Court Room was crowded at each session of Court, there being many women in attendance."

After a change of venue, Taylor was to stand trial in Lynn County for the murder of J.J. Reynolds. When the prosecution appeared without witnesses, the remaining indictment against Taylor was dismissed on September 3, 1913.

Taylor was never involved in law enforcement again. He farmed in the Lubbock area until his death in 1961. Within three years, Lubbock's aging wood courthouse was replaced by a beautiful new stone structure.

Bledsoe was elected state senator, championing the 1923 legislation that created Texas Technological College. He was a founding partner in the law firm now known as Crenshaw, Dupree & Milam.

Despite the pair of bitter defeats, Vickers established himself as a prominent trial lawyer and later as district judge. He is remembered for advising young attorneys: "If the facts are against you, argue the law. If the law is against you, argue the facts. If both law and facts are against you, jump on the opposing lawyer."

Law practice has thus changed little in the past century.

28

The Hunt Murders

Christena Stephens

In May 1942, local news spread quickly about the attempted murder of a prominent Littlefield physician who had been shot twice along the Lubbock Highway. The doctor identified a central Texas physician as the one who pulled the trigger—causing immense intrigue.

Dr. Roy Hunt, thirty-six, survived the attack. Local prosecutors brought Dr. W.R. Newton and his wife, Ruth, of Cameron, Texas, to trial for the attempted murder. In August 1943, Dr. Newton was convicted and sentenced to seven years in prison. Ruth was set to stand trial in November 1943.

Then the chilling, horrific news of a double murder hit local and national newspapers all the way to Washington, D.C. On October 26, 1943, Hunt and his wife, Mae, twenty-six, were found brutally slain in their tiny five-room brick home in Littlefield. What made the murders more shocking was the discovery that their two daughters, ages five and two, were in the home during the murders.

Law officials, after finding the battered and blood-soaked bodies, declared the double murder to be the most brutal, gruesome and fiendish crime in the history of the South Plains.

As Texas Rangers and local law enforcement officers began investigating the murders, what was discovered was horrifying. Both victims had been tied up with an assortment of materials, first separately and then together. Dr. Hunt was shot at point-blank range. He died instantly. Mae suffered for hours before dying, tied to her husband after she'd been bludgeoned.

Left: Roy and Mae Hunt, circa 1938. *Courtesy Christena Stephens.*

Right: The crime-scene photo of the nursery window through which the intruder gained access to the Hunt home in Littlefield. *Courtesy Christena Stephens.*

Roy Hunt was born in Lubbock. Among his family, George M. Hunt was one of the pioneer families in the Lubbock area, as he had first moved to the Estacado community in the 1880s. Roy's wife, Mae Franks Hunt, was from Houston. After Roy became a partner in the Littlefield Hospital, he and Mae were married in May 1937. They had two daughters, Jo Ann and Jane, who were described as the darlings of Littlefield.

As fear set in the town of Littlefield as to who had killed the couple, doors that had remained unlocked were now locked. Residents were afraid to venture out of their houses at night for fear of encountering the killer. Like most West Texas towns in 1943, Littlefield was a quiet little farm community, busy only during cotton harvest, when hundreds of migrant workers would pass through in the fall.

During the investigation, detectives discovered numerous things. One chilling fact was that the killer had entered the residence through a back window of the children's nursery and passed by their beds as they slept.

The tangled web of these murders led investigators to turn their attention to the Newtons and another suspect, forty-nine-year-old Jim Thomas. He had a criminal career dating back to 1917 from a felony theft in Sweetwater.

He had served a good portion of a twenty-five-year sentence in Nebraska for a bank robbery. He was last sent to prison for the attempted murder of Baxter Honey in Lubbock County in 1942.

It took authorities only hours to establish that Thomas was in Littlefield at the time of the murders. He was brought to Lubbock under heavy Texas Ranger guard on October 28, 1943.

Thomas was charged with Roy Hunt's murder in early 1944. Due to judicial error and appeals, he was granted three trials that kept the case tied up in courts until 1951 in Hale, Dawson and Nolan counties. He was sentenced to death twice and to life in prison once. Thomas never served time for the murder of Roy Hunt, and the State of Texas never got its opportunity for another conviction. In August 1951, he was gunned down in Durant, Oklahoma.

The tangled web of the murders continued with the trying of Dr. Newton two more times after his first conviction was overturned. Even though the Newton cases were materially weakened due to Hunt's death, Newton was found guilty of assault with intent to murder by a Swisher County jury. The jury assessed his punishment at two years in prison.

The state never prosecuted Ruth for her role in the attack.

The 1943 Hunt murders was by far one of the most heinous crimes on the South Plains, and it left many questions unanswered. It changed the way Littlefield citizens saw their own safety and mortality. More important, this odious crime robbed two daughters of knowing their parents. It robbed the Hunts of seeing their daughters growing up and living their lives until death took them naturally.

Regardless, the way the Hunts died—one quickly and the other crudely bound to her husband—reveals the brutality of an unthinkable crime for that era.

Part VII

PIONEERS AND PROMOTERS

As the head of one of the first families to settle near the Llano Estacado, Hank Smith brought both an entrepreneurial spirit and an inclusive attitude to the new land. Smith's rock home in Blanco Canyon east of present-day Crosbyton served as the gateway to the region for many years.

Another entrepreneur, George C. Wolffarth, made substantial contributions to the development of Lubbock. Still another, Roland Ponce, made a valiant effort to create an amusement park on Lubbock's east side that would reflect the pioneer spirit of the Llano.

The other subjects in this chapter became symbols. One became the iconic representative of manhood and portrayed as the "Marlboro Man." Another became one of Lubbock's most important black educators, providing sterling leadership through difficult times.

29

"UNCLE HANK" SMITH

PAUL H. CARLSON

Henry Clay Smith, known as "Uncle Hank" but born Heinrich Schmitt in Germany in 1836, came to America with two older sisters when he was fourteen. He joined relatives at Sandusky, Ohio, on the shores of Lake Erie.

Smith built barrels for several months and briefly worked as a sailor on Lake Erie. Then, in 1852, as a sixteen-year-old, he headed west to find his fortune. Over the next several years, Smith moved from one opportunity to another. He worked as a surveyor, teacher and teamster. He prospected for gold on two different occasions and fought Indians. During the Civil War, Smith found himself serving as a Confederate soldier in the Southwest. After the war, he became a teamster again and then a wagon master, and he was a cowboy for a brief time.

In the early 1870s, Smith showed up at Fort Griffin, a rough-edged town in Shackelford County that attracted cattlemen, cowboys, transients, salesmen ("drummers"), outlaws, prostitutes, adventurers and others, and the federal army maintained a garrison of soldiers near the town. At the frontier community, Smith with a government contract provided hay and wood to the military post. He also clerked in Conrad's Sutler Store at the fort.

At a New Year's Eve ball in 1874, Smith met Elizabeth Boyle, who had recently arrived at Fort Griffin from Scotland via Missouri. Just four and a half months later, on May 19, Hank and Elizabeth married. Soon, the

Elizabeth "Aunt Hank" and "Uncle" Hank Smith, circa 1902. *Courtesy Southwest Collection, Texas Tech University.*

Smiths built a hotel, called the Occidental Hotel, and settled in to host public officials, lawyers, traders, cattlemen and others.

Among those who stopped at the hotel was Charles Tasker, a young man from Philadelphia with plenty of his father's money, and a man named Jamison, supposedly an "Irish Lord." In 1876, the two newcomers hired Hank Smith to locate a ranching site for them somewhere on the West Texas plains. Smith and four others traveled to Blanco Canyon, scouted the area and returned with a favorable report.

The two would-be ranchers then hired Smith to oversee construction of a house in the canyon and collect enough cattle to start a ranching enterprise. As stonemasons began work on the house, Tasker and Jamison, who owed Smith several thousand dollars, went bankrupt. Smith, to recoup his losses, took over the ranch and cattle, and in 1877–78, he finished the large "Rock House," as it came to be called.

A year later, Hank and Elizabeth Smith, their two young children (George and Leila) and their hired man (Charley Hawse) drove wagons loaded with goods, household furnishings and equipment for a home and ranch located almost one hundred miles beyond the edge of pioneer settlement. It was a "gutsy" undertaking.

The Smiths succeeded. Elizabeth, or "Aunt Hank," as she was called, became the local postmistress, health caregiver to ill or injured cowboys and travelers, hostess for many visitors and teacher to her children. Uncle Hank tended to his cattle, put in a garden, planted fruit trees and befriended most everyone who showed up at the Rock House and his tiny Mount Blanco community.

Among those Smith befriended was a settlement of Quakers from the Midwest under the leadership of Paris Cox. In 1878, Cox had purchased some land on the Llano Estacado northwest of Smith's home and asked Uncle Hank to break out some grassland for farming and dig a well. Smith did both, and he and the Quakers became friends as well as neighbors.

On his ranch, Smith raised cattle and sheep, and one time he tried hogs. The hog business did not do well. He preferred sheep.

Smith and "Aunt Hank" had six children, five of whom lived to adulthood. Two boys, George and Robert, stayed close to the ranch, helping their dad but acquiring additional property as well. The girls (Leila, Annie and Mary) married but lived on ranches in the area.

At its peak, Hank and Elizabeth Smith's ranch consisted of ten sections of land, or about 6,400 acres. The boys helped, George preferring to run cattle and Robert preferring sheep. Hank liked his garden and fruit trees.

Hank Smith was more than a reluctant rancher. A community leader, he served as Crosby County tax assessor for a term (1886–88) and became involved in local school affairs and activities related to community service.

Hank and his family played a strong part in the development of Estacado, the Quaker community where he and Charley Hawse had dug the well. Two of the Smith children attended school there and boarded with a Quaker family, and Aunt Hank, a Presbyterian, on occasion attended Quaker meetings, but not apparently the Roman Catholic Uncle Hank. As Estacado declined in the 1890s, Smith turned to Emma, the new county seat, for business and markets.

In Blanco Canyon, his farm and ranch prospered. He died a wealthy man in 1912, and his family buried him in the Emma Cemetery.

30

George C. Wolffarth

Paul H. Carlson

George Clarence "Tildy" Wolffarth (1866–1950) was a cowboy, banker and civic leader who played a key role in the establishment of modern Lubbock.

Born near Jacksboro, Wolffarth was the fifth of eleven children. He attended school for a few months each year but was at work on the family farm and ranch most of the time.

In 1880, when he was thirteen, Wolffarth left for Mobeetie in the Texas Panhandle to work on a ranch where an older brother was employed. While working there, he acquired the nickname Tildy, which friends and relatives used thereafter. The next year, he went to work on a larger ranch, one stretching through Collingsworth and Childress counties. Here, sometime in the summer, he "went up the trail," helping to drive a herd of cattle to Kansas. Only fourteen years old, he was indeed a "cow-boy."

Once back at the ranch, Wolffarth, after the fall roundup, lived in a line camp along the Red River. As a line rider, he rode out from his camp each morning for about ten miles, turning the ranch cattle back to the appropriate pasture, before returning about dark. Blizzards, rainstorms, drought and other maladies often made the job a difficult one. And, clearly, it was a lonely one.

While he was at home in Jacksboro during the first months of 1884, Wolffarth determined to become a cowboy on his uncle's 22 Ranch in Crosby County. John Hensley, who with his brother Charles had established the ranch in 1879 at the head of McDonald Creek, had married Kate Sanders, the sister of Wolffarth's mother. Joining Wolffarth at the 22 Ranch were his cousins Will and Van Sanders.

While working for his uncle in the spring, Wolffarth went to a neighboring ranch belonging to the Kidwell brothers, whose range spread through the southwest corner of Crosby County and the southeast corner of Lubbock County, including Yellow House Canyon nearly to Buffalo Springs. On the trip, Wolffarth and some other cowboys rode up Yellow House Canyon. About where Lubbock is today, they climbed out of the valley. According to Lela D. Puryear, "as far as they could see there were antelope and mustangs grazing in the waving sea of grass."

Great blizzards and heavy snow marked the winter of 1884–85. During this time, cattle drifted as far south and west as the Pecos River. In the spring of 1885, a long and difficult roundup separated and returned the cattle to their respective owners. When the roundup was over, some of the cowboys gathered at a ranch to celebrate with a stag dance. "Half the boys," Puryear writes, "tied red bandanas on their arms and took the place of girls. There was dancing, singing and playing through the night."

That summer, Wolffarth and Van Sanders and perhaps a couple of other cowboys were camped near Estacado, which had been established about 1879. Irving Hunt, a local resident, invited the cowboys to his home to hear his sisters sing and play. Many years later, one of the sisters, Lottie Hunt, who was five at the time, became Mrs. George Wolffarth.

After his second year on the 22 Ranch, Wolffarth had a small herd of his own. Part of his salary had been paid in cattle, and in the late 1880s, with his Sanders cousins, he established a ranch next to the Western Land and Livestock Company's IOA Ranch, which controlled much of Lubbock County.

About the same time, Wolffarth got involved with the founding of present-day Lubbock. He and the Sanders brothers on several occasions visited the Nicolett Hotel in Lubbock while the building and town stood out by today's Lubbock Country Club. On one visit, Van Sanders registered at the Nicolett as being from Hong Cong, China, and Wolffarth signed in as from Kalamazoo, Michigan.

About a year later, in 1890, they joined Whit Rayner, who was building a rival town just north of present-day Jones AT&T Stadium on the Texas Tech campus. Before the end of the year, the rival towns merged into modern Lubbock, and George Wolffarth soon became county clerk. He also got involved with Lubbock real estate, banking and other businesses even as he built with his cousins a ranch north of the city.

George C. and Lottie (Hunt) Wolffarth on their wedding day, 1898. *Courtesy Southwest Collection, Texas Tech University.*

In 1909, C.J. Schroeder donated five acres for the first schoolhouse in Wolfforth, the new town named for George C. Wolffarth and his brother. *Courtesy Wolfforth Public Library.*

In 1901, Wolffarth bought a bank and with friends capitalized it as First National Bank. Three years later, he sold it to Walter Posey and O.L. Slaton, and in 1906, he helped organized Citizens National Bank, of which he was president for fourteen years.

In the 1920s, Wolffarth with his brother Estin expanded the cattle business into Terry County, where they owned and leased nearly one hundred sections of land, and then into Lynn, Bailey and Cochran counties.

As owner of several Lubbock businesses, Wolffarth was a busy civic leader, an active member of the Lubbock Business Club and the First United Methodist Church, a strong supporter of acquiring Texas Technological College and a grand ambassador of Lubbock. He died in 1950.

31

Carl "Bigun" Bradley and the Making of the Marlboro Man

Ashley Pettiet Branch

Bigun Bradley, a rugged-looking cowboy on the 6666 Ranch in Guthrie, Texas, became in 1963 the first real Marlboro Man cowboy.

It is an interesting story that grew from the desire of Marlboro advertising executives to establish a rugged, masculine image for their cigarette, a product that at the time attracted more female than male users. Looking to revamp the cigarette's image, the tobacco company in 1954 hired Chicago-based advertiser Leo Burnett. It gave him instructions to find a way to appeal to men.

At one of the subsequent but early advertising meetings, Burnett asked a group of Marlboro researchers, "What is the most masculine figure in America?" The group threw around a number of ideas, including soldiers and police officers. After someone suggested cowboys, the discussion turned immediately in that direction, and a "cowboy" image was begun.

The first men photographed for the campaign were male models merely dressed up as cowboys. The marketing team found the early advertisements lacking. They did not present the "cowboy" as a rugged, solid, self-assured and independent individual, as they wanted.

Fortunes turned for Marlboro when a Burnet art director scout, Neil McBain, came through the Rolling Plains of Texas in 1963 looking for rustic settings for a Camay soap advertisement. McBain stopped in Guthrie at the 6666 Supply House, the only general store in town. Giving orders to his cowboys at the Supply House that morning was Carl "Bigun" Bradley.

A magazine advertisement featuring the "Marlboro Man," Carl Bradley, circa 1973. *Courtesy King County Museum. Guthrie, Texas.*

McBain knew instantly he wanted the young cowboy, who stood about five feet, eleven inches and smoked only Kools, for the Marlboro campaign. Bradley had a face meant for any advertisement involving a cowboy. McBain hired Bradley on the spot.

Bigun Bradley was born on February 9, 1937, in Knox City to Carl "Banty" and Mae Bradley. Bigun began day-working around Knox and King counties before, at age fourteen, he started cowboying exclusively for the 6666. Despite the long working hours, he attended school and graduated from Knox City High School in 1956.

After high school, Bradley worked his way up from everyday cowhand to wagon boss. For as long as he could remember, his workdays started before sunup and ended long after sundown. A cowboy's schedule is not like that of a corporate executive. Cowboys like Bigun worked seven days a week, well over forty hours per week and enjoyed few days away from the job. In fact, in his more than twenty-two-year career, Bigun accepted only a few days from work each year for the Stamford Rodeo in Jones County, and in 1966, he took off two days to marry Glenda Reese.

From 1963 to 1970, Bigun Bradley was the main Marlboro Man. Sales for Marlboro cigarettes soared, and Marlboro became a bestseller. *Life* and *Look* magazines accepted full-page ads from Marlboro of a strong-jawed cowboy inviting the reader to "come to where the flavor is, come to Marlboro country." During his time as Marlboro Man, Bradley shot several hundred photographs and dozens of commercials—almost all photographed or filmed in the King County area.

In early May 1973, Bigun's father, Banty, sold a colt to a neighbor named Bill Flowers. The Flowers foreman could not handle the young colt, and he called Bigun to help. Bigun saddled the wild horse late that afternoon and rode off. Late in the evening, Bigun's wife, Glenda, called Flowers to ask if he and his family had seen Bigun.

They hadn't, but Flowers and his foreman said they would drive around to find him. They drove out to a few pastures, finding nothing, but on their way back to the ranch house, they saw a horse's leg and part of a saddle blanket sticking out from the water near the edge of a new stock tank. At midnight, Flowers drove over to see Glenda and told her that they had found the horse but not Bigun's body. On the edge of the stock tank they had found his lip ice, his gloves and a package of Kools, all dry, having been placed on the water's edge.

Local volunteers came over and began dragging the tank. Bigun's body was pulled from the tank around 2:00 a.m. There were signs of a blow over one eye and behind his ear. Bigun Bradley was pronounced dead from accidental drowning on May 10, 1973. He was thirty-six years old.

At the time, Bigun was no longer the Marlboro Man. He had stepped away from the advertising campaign two years previous. But from Bigum's start in 1963, Marlboro used only real cowboys. Customers connected with the authenticity of a man who knew how to ride, saddle his horse and strike a match on the bottom of his boot.

While there have been many a Marlboro Man, there was only the one original Marlboro cowboy, Bigun Bradley, a universal icon for what men were supposed be.

32

EDWARD C. STRUGGS

JUNE STEELE

Edward Charles Struggs (1906–1979) was principal and teacher at Dunbar High School from 1930 to 1965. Originally located at Seventeenth Street and Avenue C, the school moved to Date Avenue in 1932 and to Manhattan Heights in 1958.

Born in Wallis, Texas, in Austin County in 1906, Struggs graduated from high school in Waco. He earned a bachelor's degree from Paul Quinn College, the oldest historically black college in Texas, and an additional teaching degree from Prairie View State Normal and Industrial College.

Shortly after beginning his teaching career in Minerva, Texas, in 1925, he met Lillian Porter, a schoolteacher in Cameron, and they married in 1926.

An estimated eleven hundred African Americans lived in Lubbock in 1930, creating a permanent black community and a demand for black educators. Under such circumstances, Edward Struggs accepted a position in the city as both teacher and principal at the recently founded Dunbar School, a three-room facility in a black residential section of town. Lillian Struggs was also employed as a teacher at the school.

Struggs admitted to harboring fears about his 1930 move to Lubbock: "I was apprehensive about coming to West Texas. In fact, I didn't know what it was like. I was afraid that I wasn't going to stay….I found out as soon as I got here that Negroes were treated a lot better here in West Texas than anywhere else. That's the reason I stayed."

"Prof" E.C. Struggs was principal of Dunbar High School for thirty-five years. *Courtesy June Steele.*

At his little school, named in honor of distinguished African American poet Paul Lawrence Dunbar, enrollment in 1930 was one hundred students. Struggs described school conditions during the early 1930s as difficult, and the economic stress of the Great Depression added to the strain. He recalled that all teachers, black and white, received full paychecks in a timely fashion, but as a result of cash shortages during the depressed economic times, they often had to discount the checks' true value at banks and stores.

Struggs noted that a gap between white and black teacher salaries was significant, in Lubbock and throughout Texas. He also lamented that teaching was not as lucrative as other endeavors at the time. "I taught boys who would come to school on Monday and had made more money shining shoes in the hotels over the weekend than I would make all week teaching school. Many time I wondered if I was in the wrong profession."

Emphasizing the continuity of school funding in spite of hard economic times, Struggs praised the city of Lubbock's commitment: "Even though the town had difficulty collecting taxes, it was a priority to keep the schools going." The black community shouldered a good deal of the burden. Lacking a janitor at Dunbar, teachers and parents kept the stoves lit, and parents and students swept the floors, weeded the yards and shoveled snow or raked leaves.

Although he believed that Dunbar was shortchanged in terms of the physical plant, citing the old secondhand building and overcrowded classrooms, Struggs praised the Lubbock school board for providing black and white high school students with the same textbooks. He noted, "So many places gave Negro schools leftover, used, outdated textbooks, but it wasn't that way out here. We had the same textbooks that the white school was using."

Struggs added the eleventh grade to Dunbar in 1931 and the twelfth grade in 1932, the same year officials moved Dunbar to Date Avenue. High school offerings at Dunbar included math, history, English and general science.

The course offerings fell short of the more diverse subjects available at all-white Lubbock High School, where students as early as 1923 chose from Latin, Spanish, domestic science, vocational agriculture, home economics and orchestra.

Nonetheless, under Struggs's direction, Dunbar High School continued to grow in physical size and population, adding a marching band and an extensive athletic program. In the meanwhile, using summer vacations and other short leave periods in the 1940s, Struggs and his wife, Lillian, earned master's degrees in education at the University of Michigan. He became "Prof" Struggs.

Struggs claimed that Lubbock's black teachers experienced the same professional deference that was afforded to white teachers. He noted, for example, that white teachers, members of the Texas State Teacher's Association, and black teachers, members of the Colored Teachers State Association, met regularly together with the superintendent of schools. Such integrated meetings were unusual in Texas prior to 1963. Struggs stated, "even if a meeting was downtown at a hotel the white and colored teachers would sit together and eat together. Not like other places."

In 1965, the year Struggs retired as principal, Dunbar High School employed fifty-five teachers and enrolled over one thousand students.

Recognizing the tremendous contributions that Edward Struggs made to black education in Lubbock, the school district shortly after his retirement in 1965 opened E.C. Struggs Junior High School. Edward Struggs died in Lubbock on August 18, 1979.

33

Roland Ponce and Rimrock City

Don Abbe

During the 1950s and 1960s, Americans were deeply interested in the American West and the cowboy legend. Western-themed TV shows and movies dominated the airwaves and the box office.

Another byproduct of the Western craze was the creation of Western "towns," replicas of the typical hamlets that once dotted the West. Such attractions usually featured board sidewalks, dusty streets and false-front wood buildings. The recreations were intended to be tourist destinations and often featured regularly scheduled gunfights, Western-themed miniature golf courses and other such activities.

In Lubbock, the Western phenomenon came relatively late. It was a place called Rimrock City. The developer, Roland Ponce, built the "city" on the far eastern edge of Lubbock, just outside Loop 289, where it intersects with East Fiftieth Street. It was located on the west side of the shallow valley of the upper Brazos River.

Ponce served as president of Rimrock City and Zoological Gardens. Investors and officers were R.B. Quest, vice-president; Kent Clark, vice-president; and Mrs. V.V. Clark, A. E. Quest, Carl Clark, George Turner, Ira Williams and Russell Simpkins, officers.

The land, 177 acres, was secured in 1964. Construction began on the first phase of the project soon after, and the complex was opened on May 22, 1965. Many of the buildings and materials were brought from another, but failed, Rimrock City located between Midland and Odessa.

The Red Garter Saloon and Entertainment Center at Rimrock City, circa 1965. *Photo by Rollin Herald, courtesy Southwest Collection, Texas Tech University.*

On opening day, Rimrock City contained a variety of structures and attractions. They included a saloon/restaurant (The Red Garter), a bank (which was robbed daily), a livery stable, a general mercantile store, a lawyer's office, a barbershop, a doctor's office, a blacksmith shop, a small chapel (which held Sunday morning services) and an eighteen-hole miniature golf course. Each of the town buildings was a fully functioning structure, complete with antique furnishings and equipment needed to make them "authentic" Western places. The blacksmith could shoe local horses when requested.

The complex also contained a reptile garden, a two-mile horseback riding trail, a "model" 1863 train locomotive and a track on which it ran, as well as a private picnic area that was available to visitors. Stagecoach rides were likewise available.

Ponce and the other officers hired C.W. Yeats of Houston to serve as curator of the Zoological Garden. They purchased an elephant and located it in the zoo. They hoped the pachyderm would be a major attraction and draw folks from far and wide. To feed the elephant, Ponce got Bill McAlister and Lew Dee on their morning radio show in April 1965 to help raise money to provide food and a good home at the zoo for Norma (the elephant).

Snakes and other wildlife, including bears, buffalo, an ostrich and dolphins, were among the zoo's many occupants.

The developers hoped to get sponsorships for Rimrock City, with the local businesses taking the lead. The effort did not work.

Plans for a second phase of construction included an eighteen-hole, regulation PGA golf course, a frontier cavalry post and museum, an indoor/outdoor shooting range, a larger "frontier" restaurant, a trout fishing pond and a convention auditorium seating five hundred people. None of it came to pass.

Fate was unkind to Rimrock City. America's interest in all things Western began to fade in the mid-1960s, just when the town was trying to expand. Besides, Lubbock, with a population of 141,000 people, was not large enough to provide a "market" for a tourist attraction like Rimrock City. Attendance was modest and dropped off dramatically after a few months of operation.

Rimrock City closed its doors in late 1966 or early 1967. Norma the elephant found a new home, and the site entered a long period of decay. The buildings and golf course slowly began to deteriorate. The "alligator" pit (a cement pond) grew only mosquitoes. Many of the buildings, including the chapel and concession stand, were demolished or sold and moved.

By 1971, the townsite had come under lease to Mr. and Mrs. Charles Thompson. By 1977, it was crumbling into oblivion and looked like an Old West ghost town. In 1998, it became the property of Brice Chapman, a trick roper and farrier.

Although the old townsite has pretty much vanished, Chapman, whose father shod horses at Rimrock City during its heyday, has turned Norma's house into a blacksmith/horseshoeing shop and the headquarters building into his office. He raises cattle where one can still see remnants of the miniature golf course, building foundations and a wall or two that still stand.

People who drive by the site each day can only imagine what turned out to be an ill-timed attempt to bring the Old West back to life along the upper reaches of the Brazos River in Yellow House Canyon.

Part VIII

LONELY PLACES

In a sense, this part deals with lonely places, once booming communities but now virtually ghost towns. From Estacado, the first town on the Llano, to Becton, to Emma, the essays reveal the importance of timing and location in a community's history.

In spite of living in a large town, for thirty-two Japanese American residents, the Llano Estacado became one of the loneliest places in the world at the outbreak of World War II. Caught in the backlash against Japan, these people were relocated out of the region, never to return.

34
Estacado, Texas

Paul H. Carlson

Estacado was the seat of Crosby County for about five years, after which it lost a county seat vote to Emma, and a steady decline set in.

The little Quaker farming and ranching community began in the fall of 1879, when Paris Cox and his family with three additional families settled on land Cox had purchased in 1877 and 1878. Cox built a sod house for his family. The three others spent a tough winter, 1879–80, in tents. In the spring, the tent-dwelling families gave up in disgust and returned to their former homes in Indiana.

Cox hung on. He planted crops in the spring and through letters encouraged other Quakers to join his family. Dr. William Hunt stopped at the Cox farm that summer and described what he observed: "I visited [Cox] in August and September 1880. I saw corn, oats, millet, sorghum, melons, Irish potatoes, sweet potatoes, and garden vegetables—all did well." He stuck around.

In the fall, other Quakers arrived, and within two years, ten families had settled in the community, named Marietta (or Maryetta) in honor of Cox's wife, Mary. Later, after it was learned that a Marietta post office already existed in Texas, leaders changed the name to Estacado. The community, located on the Lubbock-Crosby County line and along present-day Farm Road 1527, continued to grow. People lived in dugouts and sod homes at first, but as lumber arrived in freight wagons from Colorado City, they built wood-frame houses.

In 1882, Emma Hunt began education classes for Quaker children. She taught first in a dugout but in 1884 shifted to a Quaker meetinghouse that had been built. A post office was established in 1884. William Hunt became the postmaster.

When Crosby County was organized in 1886, Estacado, although a part of the little town dribbled over into Lubbock County, became the county seat. Until a courthouse was built a couple of years later, county officials kept records and offices in dugouts and tiny, shack-like buildings around town. Pioneer settlers continued to arrive and establish farms in the area. The Estacado population grew as farmers, aided by Cox and his knowledge of available land parcels, secured property, planted crops and traded in town. Business owners arrived as well.

In 1890, Estacado claimed nearly two hundred residents. It had, wrote one visitor, "two general stores, a hotel, a lawyer's office, a newspaper, the county courthouse, and a meeting house which doubled for church and school." The school Miss Hunt had started was now taught by two public school teachers who provide education to at least thirty-two pupils. In addition, Central Plains Academy, the first college on the Llano Estacado, began operations in 1890. Unfortunately, it lasted only two years.

There was other troubling news in 1890. The newspaper editor, John W. Murray, who had arrived in 1887, used his paper, the *Crosby County News*, to advertise the town. Quaker farmers in the area opposed the "boosterism." Area cattlemen and cowboys likewise opposed Murray's town promotion. The region was cattle country, and they didn't want farmers taking up grazing land.

Cowboys also wanted a saloon and probably got one or two, but the record is mute. Nonetheless, during construction of the courthouse in 1888, some of the cowboys in defiance of the law lounged on lumber piles intended for the courthouse and gambled at poker. T. Lindsay Baker in his book *Ghost Towns of Texas* writes that the sheriff's "officers paid only passing notice to most of them, and Estacado in time gained a reputation for law and order."

Despite the town's growth and favorable reputation, difficulties mounted. Cox died in 1888, and the community lost his leadership. In addition, R.L. Stringfellow and H.E. Hume, who operated a general merchandise store in Estacado, moved their business to land they owned near the center of Crosby County. Murray, who because of his "booming" of Estacado was feeling more and more isolated in the Quaker community, joined them.

Although Estacado prospered for a decade in the 1880s, the town's decline came quickly after 1891. In that year, the busy little village lost a

This 1936 Texas centennial marker stands in the center of what was once the thriving Quaker community of Estacado. *Courtesy Ellen Carlson.*

county seat vote to Emma, the town that Stringfellow, Hume and Murray had established. Afterward, many Quakers left Estacado. Some headed to the new village of Lubbock some fifteen miles away. Others returned to their former homes in the Middle West, and still others relocated to the new community of Friendswood, southeast of Houston.

A drought in 1892–93 and a severe grasshopper invasion further decimated the population. The post office closed in 1918. In the 1920s, the town had two churches, a couple of stores, a rural school and a dozen residences. In 1930, the population stood at sixty-five, but ten years later, some eighty-five inhabitants called Estacado home.

In 2020, all that remains are a couple of buildings, a historical marker and the old Estacado cemetery south of the former town.

35

Becton, Texas

Paul H. Carlson

Becton, Texas, located in the far northeast corner of Lubbock County, experienced—has witnessed—a rare history. It began with W.E. Bledsoe.

About 1891, Bledsoe, who in 1886 had come to the area to round up wild horses, established something of a community on his ten-section Three Circle Ranch. He wanted a school for his children and thus built a one-room building about three miles southeast of the ranch homestead. Soon other children were attending the little Bledsoe School. Located one and a quarter miles north and one mile west of the current Becton townsite, it became the Bledsoe Independent School District, and the village nearby became known as Bledsoe.

Mary Louise McDonald writes that in "those days in this wide open country there were no landmarks, and the blizzards were frequent." As a precaution, she states, school supporters plowed a furrow from the schoolhouse "straight to each patron's home so that in case of a storm the children would not get lost."

In 1917, when he applied for a post office for the community, grocery store owner E.H. Moody discovered there was already at that time a Texas town called Bledsoe (but not the present town of Bledsoe on the state line in Cochran County). Thereupon, he used the name Becton, after Abner M. Becton, an early settler who had come to the area about 1895. Moody became the first and only postmaster, and his post office operated into the 1940s, after which the postal service closed it.

In its early days, Becton—or Bledsoe until 1917—residents got their supplies from Amarillo. Cattlemen drove animals to market there and returned with clothing, foodstuffs and other items. Teamsters hauled coal for cooking and heating from Amarillo until the Santa Fe Railroad reached Lubbock in 1909.

After Mr. Becton donated land for a new school building, officials moved the school to town. Until consolidation with Idalou schools in the 1930s, it remained the Bledsoe Independent School District. Originally, churchgoers met in the school building, but in 1915, a Baptist church was started. Two years later, a Church of Christ congregation began holding services, and in 1927, a Methodist church opened. None survive in 2020.

In 1923, a new, large brick schoolhouse opened. More than sixty children, representing all grades, attended, and four or five teachers taught them. In the 1920s, the school fielded a good high school boys' basketball team.

Isolated, but located in a rich farming area, the little town of Becton prospered for a time, particularly as irrigation increased. Grain sorghum, wheat and especially cotton became the principal crops in the area and replaced ranching as the major business activity.

For several years, Becton hosted a July 4 Independence Day, celebration. As part of it in 1924, local leaders sponsored a rodeo that, recalled Arno Struve, was "participated in by all local people." One of the events included

A 1928 view of Becton from the top of the bridge looking east. *Courtesy Ute Becton.*

a "wild cow milking contest in which the milkers held beer bottles into which they must 'squirt' the milk."

In 1928, the Fort Worth & Denver Railway built a line through Becton to Lubbock. Perhaps to accommodate the citizens of the little town, railroad construction workers cut a shallow trough in which to lay its tracks on the western edge of town and built a bridge (viaduct) over the tracks.

The big structure was ninety-five feet long, twenty-five feet high and wide enough for automobiles and trucks to pass by one another. Ed Bledsoe recalls that he was "always getting into mischief down under the viaduct." He remembers that on Sundays "all the kids" from the three churches "went there between Sunday School and church."

The large wooden structure served Becton well until 1994. The railroad had taken up the tracks by then, the viaduct was becoming unsafe and it was no longer needed. It came down.

The railroad brought a few new residents, but the Great Depression stymied further growth. In the meantime, according to historian Greg Bledsoe, in 1936, Becton boasted of a post office, three grocery stores (two of which maintained gasoline pumps), three churches, a blacksmith shop, a cotton gin and a grain elevator. About 150 people lived in Becton.

Like many small towns, Becton did not last. Its population remained pretty stable into the 1970s, but better roadways as a result of the expanding farm-to-market road system and improved automobiles and trucks after World War II contributed to small-town decline.

The Becton Grocery with its "filling station," for example, was in 1967 the only food retailer remaining. It had been in existence for thirty-five years but was about to close. Fortunately for local citizens, Morris A. Waters, a carpenter, cabinetmaker and homebuilder in Becton, leased the building and kept it open. Morris and his wife repainted the store, gave it a general facelift and brought in what the *Lorenzo Tribune* called "new stock."

Eventually, it closed, and Becton continued its decline. Few people live there today.

36

Emma, Crosby County, Texas

Paul H. Carlson

For twenty years, Emma was the seat of Crosby County. Located about five miles straight south of Ralls, the town both lived and died as a result of rival communities fighting to become the center of county government.

Emma was named for Emma Savior, who later became the wife of general merchandiser R.L. Stringfellow. Its story began in Estacado, the Quaker community along the Lubbock-Crosby County line, in the late-1880s. Estacado was the county seat of Crosby County. But there were problems. First, Texas law required county seats to be near the geographic center of the county. Estacado was nowhere near the required location.

Second, in 1887, John W. Murray, a newspaperman and town promoter, arrived in Estacado. He established the *Crosby County News* and used his paper, like many town boosters, to "boom" Estacado. Murray's articles and editorials praised Crosby County, showing, as John C. Jenkins, wrote, "the many opportunities offered the new settler." His reports "created a great deal of interest in Estacado and Crosby County" from both prospective farmer-settlers and land speculators. If Jenkins is correct, Murray sent out "several hundred copies" of the paper "all over the United States each week."

Quakers, who dominated Estacado's population of about two hundred people, opposed such "boosterism" and clashed with Murray. They got help from area cattlemen and their cowboys who did not want farmer-settlers coming into their ranching country. At the same time, Estacado merchants Stringfellow and his cousin H.E. Hume had determined to leave Estacado.

Entrepreneurs who realized the problem of Estacado's geographical relationship to the center of the county, they purchased a section of land, moved their business—Stringfellow and Hume General Merchandise—to their land and encouraged others to join them.

Murray and his wife, Rebecca T. Murray, becoming increasingly isolated in Estacado, joined them. In fact, it may have been Murray who took the lead in starting the new town and, in doing so, encouraged the merchants to purchase land in the south center of the county for a new town. Whatever the truth may be, Murray and his newspaper had lost the support of local Quaker farmers, who found his boosterism unbearable. Moreover, a struggle of sorts was developing between a growing number of non-Quaker farmers in the area and the original Quaker settlers.

In any case, in December 1890, Murray with his family and printing equipment moved to the new townsite. In early 1891, Stringfellow and Hume also relocated to Emma, as it was now called, and "soon several families," according the Jenkins, had transferred to the new town.

Led by Murray, Stringfellow and Hume, town builders quickly began agitating to move the county seat from Estacado to Emma. They succeeded—quickly. In a county-seat election on October 14, 1891, Emma received 109 votes, a placed called "Section 1" east of Emma got 19 votes and Estacado had only 3 votes recorded.

Emma grew rapidly, but it was never large. The *Texas Almanac* indicated that two hundred people lived there in 1904, and the town's population may have reached five hundred inhabitants in 1910, although one questionable report suggests a population of nearly seven hundred people. As Emma grew, Estacado declined. Cattlemen and cowboys were delighted, for they did not want farmers, including Quaker farmers, in the area. In fact, as workers at a cost of $3,000 dismantled the courthouse in Estacado before moving it to the new seat of government, cowboys sat on the growing stack of lumber from the carefully disassembled building (even the nails were saved) smoking cigarettes, chewing tobacco and celebrating its demise.

Emma became a "cowboy" town. Someone described it as a "typical western cowboy town, and [it] was rather wild when compared to [Estacado]." Henry Clay "Uncle Hank" Smith in 1912 wrote that Emma "had a tarantula emporium and a drug store which made two saloons, and for rotten dope labeled out to mankind, [the town] was a glittering success." Smith also said, "In those days the courthouse was a merry old place, and smelled more like the fumes of a booze factory rather than a temple of justice."

This attractive sign on State Highway 207 marks the approximate location of Emma. *Courtesy Ellen Carlson.*

The town was not all about liquor. Stringfellow and Humes operated their general merchandise store. There was a post office and other businesses. Joe and Margaret With ran a hotel in Emma, and as the town grew, they added to their building. They catered to teamsters, farmers, lawyers, cattlemen and cowboys, judges and "drummers."

The Church of Christ held Sunday services. Joe Day of Floyd County and Charlie Smith of Lockney came to direct church services, sometimes coming together.

The end of Emma came in 1911, when the town lost a vote to Crosbyton for county seat. Not long after the election, four big traction engines (tractors), "30 men, and 22 mules constituted a caravan that moved businesses, buildings, and residences across the prairie to Crosbyton." And Emma just disappeared.

37

The Santa Fe Railroad and Japanese Americans of Clovis

Dolores Mosser and Sammie Simpson

The Japanese surprise attack on America's air and naval forces at Pearl Harbor in Hawaii propelled the United States into World War II. The attack also initiated an unfortunate chapter in American history: governmental restrictions on American-born Japanese citizens and Japanese nationals who lived and worked in the United States.

These events are thought to have happened far from the Llano Estacado, but in fact, World War II restrictions of Japanese Americans played out only one hundred miles from Lubbock in Clovis, New Mexico.

Clovis was an important Santa Fe "railroad town." After the town was founded in 1909, Santa Fe began to relocate Japanese railroad workers and their families from Arizona and California. A small community of Japanese Americans and Japanese nationals was housed in a one-story wooden building located east of the railroad roundhouse. Apartments in the building surrounded an interior courtyard, where the residents grew vegetables. In turn, the produce, and trinkets from Japan, were sold to Clovis residents.

Japanese children attended both public and private schools. Besides working as railroad laborers, the Japanese also found employment as janitors and messengers. By the 1930s, the Japanese laborers were promoted to highly skilled jobs as Santa Fe machinists. In 1941, thirty-two Japanese—fifteen adults and seventeen children—lived in Clovis: the Kimura, Ebihara, Okazaki and Hatae families.

The Santa Fe Depot in Clovis, New Mexico, c. 1960. *Courtesy Portal to Texas History, (https://texashistory.unt.edu/ark:/67531/metapth28605/: accessed December 10, 2019), University of North Texas Libraries, https://texashistory.unt.edu; crediting Museum of the American Railroad.*

John Cully tells the story of the Japanese of Clovis in *High Plains History* by John McAlavy and Harold Kilmer (1979). "The railroad valued the Japanese as dependable and loyal workers," Cully stated.

The war years were difficult times for the Japanese in America. They suffered from reprisals by angry Americans, citizen-review boards and placement in internment camps established in seven states. Hostilities against the Japanese in Clovis were real, and the Japanese American citizens had little local protection—partly because the New Mexico National Guard, including young men from eastern New Mexico, were sent to the Philippines to battle invading Japanese forces.

"On the afternoon of Pearl Harbor [December 7, 1941]," wrote Cully, "W.R. Harrison, the Mechanical Superintendent over the Clovis shops, rushed down from his office in Amarillo [because] the Japanese presented the Santa Fe with a difficult problem, for they worked in jobs of military significance." This division of the railroad, called the Belen Cutoff, was a major artery to the West Coast. Therefore, special attention was given to ensure its security. Harrison was directed to oversee the relocation and the safety of their hardworking Japanese employees and their families.

Japanese Americans were well aware of their situation due to the war. Officials instructed them to stay in their homes.

On January 22, 1942, Everett Grantham, a former Clovis resident and the U.S. attorney for the Federal Judicial District of New Mexico, was briefed on the Clovis Japanese situation. He learned that the Alien Enemy Hearing Board ordered the removal of the former Santa Fe employees and their families to an undisclosed location.

Grantham traveled to Clovis to implement the relocation. Upon his arrival, he was told how the Japanese were "menaced by the populace" and "very much in fear of their lives." U.S. Border Patrol agents guarded the Japanese until midnight on January 23, when they were moved to the Fort Stanton Military Reservation near Lincoln, New Mexico. The day before, Richard Dick Masura Kimura was born, but his birth was not registered in Curry County.

The Japanese of Clovis were settled in an abandoned CCC camp, known as Old Raton Ranch, ten miles from Fort Stanton. For the next year, the former Clovis residents lived on fourteen acres of land with several rundown buildings. Once again, they were resolute in their plight. They planted flowers and gardens for fresh food but endured destitution and isolation.

The Santa Fe Railroad placed the Japanese workers on "leave of absence" but allowed them to correspond with Clovis officials. Cully wrote, "The Japanese displayed no bitterness over their fate, but they were worried and dismayed." Their greatest concern was the education of the children. At first, children attended school in Capitan, but they were removed due to local hostilities there. Amy Ebihara, who had attended Clovis High School, became the camp teacher. R.E. Marshall, her former high school principal, sent books to the new school.

In December 1942, the Clovis Japanese were removed from New Mexico to camps in Arizona and Utah. After the war, a few returned to Japan, but the remainder found jobs in Utah, Colorado and Kansas.

None of the Clovis Japanese Americans returned to their former home on the High Plains, and an apartment compound in which they had lived, called "Jap Town" by most people in Clovis, was demolished.

Perhaps the one bright spot to the sorry situation was that the Santa Fe Railroad's Railroad Retirement Board awarded the Clovis Japanese American machinists retirement annuities.

Part IX

ETHNIC ENCLAVES AND INTEGRATION

As in many parts of the country, especially in the South, life for minorities has generally been difficult. On the Llano Estacado, African Americans remained segregated well into the twentieth century.

But Lubbock's black community, with strong leadership from such men as Edward C. Struggs (see chapter 32) and Dr. J.A. Chatman, worked hard to overcome adversity by establishing its own schools and hospital.

The chapter begins with a review of an African American cowboy who became one of West Texas's most respected ranchers and who overcame prejudice against him through hard work. It ends with the story of German-speaking Mennonites who are achieving the same end in the same way.

38

DANIEL WEBSTER "80 JOHN" WALLACE

JOHN T. "JACK" BECKER

On a cold March morning in 1876, fifteen-year-old Daniel Webster Wallace stole away from home in Fayette County, Texas, to become a cowboy. Numerous times, he had seen cowboys driving cattle past his home and often thought that life on horseback was more agreeable than the future he saw before him—a life of farmwork, picking cotton and hoeing corn.

Finding his way to some cowboys camping near his home, young Wallace convinced the trail boss to give him a try. The boss agreed to hire him on condition he prove himself by breaking a particularly wild horse. Years later, Wallace remembered digging his feet into the stirrups and holding on to the saddle horn as hard as he could, for he was determined to become a cowboy.

Successfully riding the wild bucking horse earned Wallace a job as wrangler of the remuda. The outfit he joined trailed a herd through Buffalo Gap, Texas, to "good grass" near the Runnels-Taylor County line. For his efforts, he earned $1.50.

Wallace, who was African American, worked for many cattlemen who later became well known in the history of ranching in West Texas. First, he "cowboyed" for noted cattleman and Indian fighter Sam Gholson. Next, he worked for Sam Nunn, whom he helped move a herd all the way from East Texas to Sand Rock Springs near present Snyder in Scurry County.

After working for Nunn, Wallace worked for another celebrated cattleman, Clay Mann, who at one time owned more cattle than anyone else in Texas. Wallace joined Mann's outfit when Mann owned a ranch in Coleman County

Daniel Webster Wallace, circa 1931. *Courtesy Southwest Collection, Texas Tech University.*

on the banks of Indian Creek where it empties into the Jim Ned. A stone wall and corrals that Wallace helped to build still stand and are part of the modern-day Rafter-3 Ranch headquarters.

Wallace worked for Mann for eleven years and developed a close working relationship with his employer. Wallace's hard work, dependability and willingness to take on additional responsibility soon advanced him to the position of foreman. His long relationship with Mann also led to his nickname, "80 John." Someone once said that Daniel Wallace had worked so long for Mann that he probably had Mann's "80" branded on him. Wallace didn't seem to mind, and the name stuck. He was known as 80 John for the rest of his life.

After selling the ranch in Coleman County, Mann, in the early 1880s, started a ranch in Mitchell County. Indian raids were still common there. During a three-year period, the ranch lost horses to Comanche raiders. One year, 80 John lost his favorite horse, but he stayed on and helped Clay Mann build a ranch on top of the Llano Estacado. Later, Mann started a cattle operation in Mexico and 80 John moved there to help start a ranch. But after a furious Indian raid killed Mann's brother, 80 John, with everyone else associated with Mann's Mexico operation, returned to Texas. Wallace remained in Texas for the rest of his life.

Before he died, Mann encouraged 80 John to purchase cattle and land on his own, which Wallace did beginning in 1885. That year, he purchased two sections of land in Mitchell County near the little community of Loraine.

Unable to read or write, and very much wanting to do so, 80 John went to school during the winter—when he had time to study. While in school, he met his future wife, Laura Dee Owen, who also attended the little school. The couple married in 1888, moved to the land 80 John owned and began their life together. They raised four children, all of whom received a college education.

At first, 80 John Wallace supplemented his family's income by working part time for other ranchers. He worked hard, saved his money and slowly increased his cattle herd and landholdings. By 1917, he had become a well-respected citizen of Mitchell County and a member of the Texas and Southwestern Cattle Raiser's Association.

Unlike a lot of cattlemen, Wallace held on to his ranch during the darkest days of the Great Depression in the 1930s. By the time of his death on March 28, 1939, he had developed a well-managed ranch totaling sixteen sections of land and a large cattle herd. He leased some of his land to tenant farmers. His record is a remarkable one. Wallace was one of the few African American cowboys who became a large-scale rancher in West Texas.

Today, the house Wallace built on his ranch, the "Triangle D" in Mitchell County, can be seen at the National Ranching Heritage Center on the Texas Tech campus in Lubbock. But the large cattle-ranching operation Daniel Webster "80 John" Wallace and his wife, Laura, built over a lifetime together is owned and operated by one of their descendants.

39

Desegregation of Lubbock Schools

June Steele

Schooling in Lubbock started in the courthouse, homes, churches and privately owned buildings beginning as early as the town's founding in 1890.

The dramatic rise in Lubbock's population in the 1920s, credited to the boom in cotton growing, prompted Lubbock's citizens, black and white, to consider more formal efforts at educating the region's youth. Funds raised during the important 1920s enabled construction of a grand high school on Nineteenth Street known as Tom S. Lubbock High School. The beautiful facility opened to white students in 1932.

Education for African American students took a different path. In the 1920s, black students met in churches, including Mount Gilead, established in 1917. But continuing growth prompted black citizens in 1922 to appeal for funds from the Lubbock School Board for a school. None was forthcoming. Thus, black parents raised money, purchased a lot and constructed a two-room building on Seventeenth Street. In the fall of 1923, the school opened and was christened the Paul Lawrence Dunbar School. In 1932, the Dunbar School added the twelfth grade.

Growth of Lubbock to the south led in the 1950s to construction of a new high school at Forty-Seventh Street and Indiana—Monterey.

In 1954, the U.S. Supreme Court handed down the momentous *Brown v. Board of Education of Topeka* decision, stating that segregation in public schools

Mount Gilead Church was one of the first places used in Lubbock for teaching African American students. *Courtesy June Steele.*

created unequal conditions between white and black schools and ordering that all public schools in the South be integrated.

Monterey High School opened its doors on September 7, 1955, but the beautiful, modern school welcomed white students only. A third high school to admit only whites, Coronado High on Thirty-Fourth Street, received students for the 1965–66 school year, but it did not completely meet the needs of Lubbock's continuing growth.

Then, Estacado High School opened for the 1967–68 school year on the northeast side of town near Mackenzie Park. Estacado was to receive students from families building homes in the area of Lubbock Country Club. Those enrollees never materialized as the 1970 tornado tore through the area, leaving houses dismantled and homeowners looking to live elsewhere. Estacado became a minority school; little changed at all-black Dunbar High.

The lack of racial integration in Lubbock schools originated with a city ordinance in 1923. It limited the African American residential community to an area south of Nineteenth Street and east of Avenue A. Like students all over the American South, black and white children simply attended the schools in their respective neighborhoods. Thus, black children were kept out of white schools by the historic boundaries of their school districts.

African Americans in Lubbock remained largely entrenched in the historically black section of town known as the "East Side." By virtue of the residential boundaries for school attendance, black children who after *Brown v. Board of Education* were now eligible to attend a white school were excluded by residence.

School districts employed many tactics to avoid integration: starting integration in the first grade guaranteed that full integration would not be achieved for twelve years. Some schools admitted black students but kept them in separate classes from white students. Eventually, the Lubbock school system employed the controversial method of busing white students to black neighborhood schools and busing black students to white neighborhood schools. Busing of students across town achieved measurable success. By 1968, Lubbock claimed that 47 percent of the black children in the school system attended schools other than the four previously all-black institutions of Dunbar High, Struggs Junior High, Phillis Wheatley Elementary and Ella Iles Elementary.

Representatives from the Office of Civil Rights in Washington, D.C., came in 1969 to investigate the Lubbock school system. A year later, the Justice Department brought a legal suit against the Texas Education Agency and the Lubbock Independent School District, alleging that, although LISD had achieved crossover in some previously all-white schools, it had failed to eliminate its "dual school structure" at the primarily black schools, Dunbar, Struggs, Wheatley and Iles.

Slow but constant efforts on the part of the school district prevented disaster. A temporary solution was found by redrawing the attendance lines at Dunbar High School and increasing white enrollment by 263 and Hispanic enrollment by 82 for the 1970–71 school year. Other changes implemented soon after involved Struggs Junior High, which lost its ninth grade and began offering only seventh and eighth grades. At Dunbar High School, the first integrated senior class graduated in the spring of 1972.

Desegregation of public schools led to loss of employment for some of America's black administrators and teachers. In Lubbock, however, teaching staff began to integrate in 1964 and black teachers in Lubbock all retained their jobs. Still, the African American community described the integration process as agonizingly slow.

A sad consequence of integrating Lubbock schools was the slow, steady toll it took on the cohesiveness of the African American community by eroding its anchor institution, Dunbar High School, converted to a junior high in 1993.

40

Dr. Chatman and the Chatman Hospital

Sally Still Abbe

Joseph Alvin Chatman, the second African American physician in Lubbock, dedicated his life to the improvement of medical facilities for underserved citizens of Lubbock and the South Plains and of race relations. Dr. Chatman came to Lubbock in 1939, arriving with seven dollars in his pocket.

A Texas native, Chatman graduated from Meharry Medical College in Nashville, Tennessee, in 1926. Because he could not afford textbooks, he said, "I used to wait until the other boys went out courtin' and borrowed their books to study while they were gone."

He practiced medicine in Mexia, Texas, before moving to Lubbock, where he opened a practice on the east side. Because he was denied privileges at city hospitals (where African American patients also were unwelcome), Chatman in 1945 built a hospital at East Twenty-Third Street and Cedar Avenue. Construction was of "cast stone" concrete blocks poured on site by Dr. Chatman and his two young sons.

In addition to sixteen patient beds, the hospital had treatment rooms and a labor and delivery facility with eight bassinets. Most important, it contained two operating rooms, where white surgeons often performed life-saving surgery on their black patients from across West Texas. Dr. Chatman also opened a nursing school, and the nurses' dormitory still stands on Date Avenue near the hospital.

On Juneteenth Day 1949, the *Lubbock Avalanche-Journal* honored Chatman as the "most valuable negro citizen of Lubbock." The newspaper reported

Postcard view of Chatman Hospital in Lubbock, circa 1950. *Courtesy Sally Still Abbe.*

that he was the most respected African American in the city, citing his presidency of the Commonwealth Club and chairmanship of the World War II War Bond Committee. He was "a contributor to all negro churches" and "teacher of the Adult Bible class which meets in the Ritz Theater."

Dr. Chatman gave frequent lectures. In 1949, the *Avalanche-Journal* reported on one of the talks, stating, "Appeal Made by Negro Leader Here for Better Understanding." Chatman "made a stirring appeal for a better understanding and better educational facilities for his race.…As expensive as you may think it is to educate any Negro, it is far more expensive to leave him ignorant."

As Dr. Chatman's medical practice grew, so did his stature as a citizen of Lubbock, the region and the state of Texas. His fellow African American physicians elected him president of the Lone Star State Medical Society, an organization of black Americans in the health field. He authored a history of that organization, which was published in 1959.

Texas governors appointed Chatman to the President's White House Conference on Youth in 1960 and to the Conference on the Aged in 1964. In Lubbock, he chaired the board of the Negro Boys Club and served on the City Hall building committee and the Red Cross disaster committee.

Active in politics, Chatman was the first black to be an official in the Lubbock County Democratic Party and served several times as a delegate to

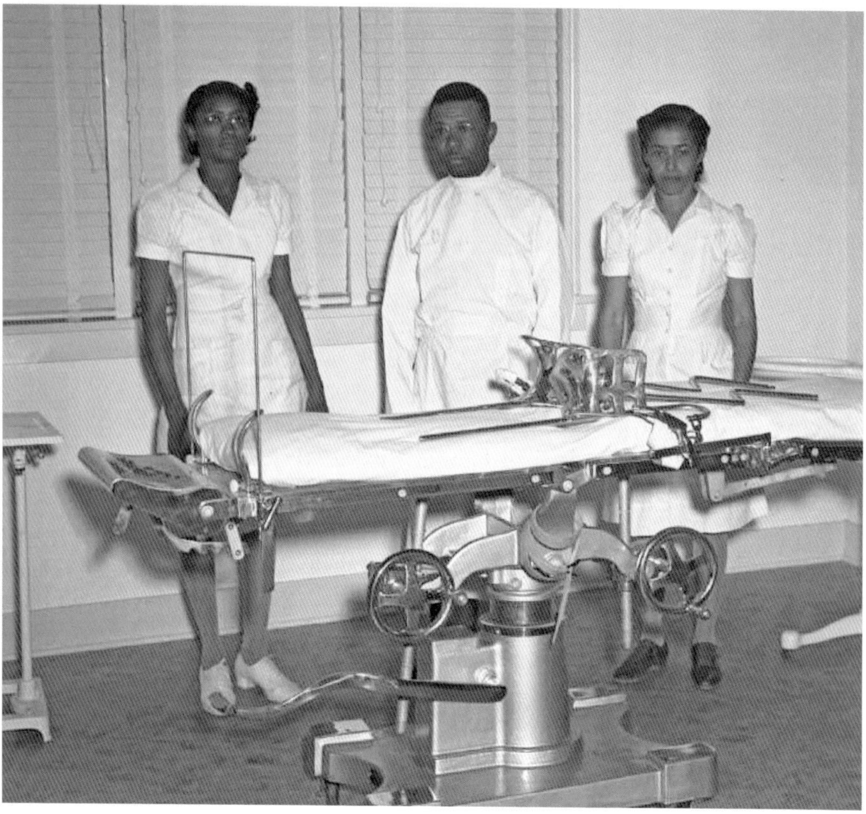

Dr. Chatman and two of his nurses pose in the operating room in the Chatman Hospital. *Courtesy Sally Still Abbe.*

the party's state convention. Governor John Connally appointed him to the board of Texas Southern University in May 1963. Eventually, he served on the medical staff at St. Mary's Hospital, an opportunity closed to members of his race for many years.

The larger Lubbock community respected Dr. Chatman, and more than 150 "friends, associates and business men" attended a testimonial dinner in his honor in April 1963.

Referring to him as "one of Lubbock's leading citizens for more than 20 years," the *Lubbock Avalanche-Journal* on January 13, 1967, carried news of Dr. Chatman's sudden death the previous evening. He was only sixty-three years old. His services were held in First Methodist Church to accommodate the more than 1,400 friends and associates who wished to honor him. The paper indicated that Dr. Chatman was a man of "many firsts." It continued: "Doctor Chatman's principal 'first' was in bridging the communication gap between the Negro and white residents of this city." In recognition of his contributions to the community, the Lubbock City Council a month later named a vacant lot at East Twenty-Eighth Street and Juniper Avenue Chatman Park.

After Dr. Chatman's death, the Chatman Hospital building became the Presbyterian Center, an outreach effort serving the East Lubbock community. Later abandoned, the building burned in 1987, leaving only the "fireproof" concrete-block walls. The building was restored to its original appearance through the efforts of a multicultural group of Lubbock citizens led by Dr. Chatman's son Harold Chatman. Many of this group had known and admired Dr. Chatman and were determined to see his legacy live on.

In 1993, University Medical Center reopened the building as Chatman Memorial Clinic. The facility is now operated by the Community Health Clinic of Lubbock (CHCL), which serves more than twenty-five thousand otherwise underserved patients annually through its eight medical and dental clinics in Lubbock. Like Dr. Joseph Alvin Chatman, CHCL's mission is to provide quality primary and preventative healthcare services to those in need.

41

Dunbar High School and State Athletic Championships

Paul H. Carlson

The former Dunbar High School in Lubbock enjoyed an enviable record in both academics and athletics. Indeed, in football, basketball and track, the school won several state championships.

In 1920, a small school for African American children opened in the Flats neighborhood—the first school in Lubbock for black students. Three years later, citizens, led by Will Sedberry and Oscar Iles, built a school in the same area at Seventeenth Street and Avenue C. A few years later, students and officials named the school for Paul Laurence Dunbar, an American poet, novelist and playwright of the late nineteenth and early twentieth centuries. Although among the first black American poets to gain national recognition, Dunbar died from tuberculosis at age thirty-four.

Enough students attended Dunbar School that officials expanded the building in 1928. William H. Wilson (the principal), Mrs. Wilson and Ella Carruthers (who married Oscar Iles) had been the teachers since 1923. In 1930, they taught 227 students.

Edward C. "Prof" Struggs became principal in 1930, and he moved to add grades eleven and twelve, thus making Dunbar a four-year high school. Two years later, the school held its first high school graduation. Also in 1932, officials relocated Dunbar to a new building on East Twenty-Sixth Street and Date Avenue. Attendance continued to grow through the next two decades, and in 1948, about 873 students enrolled for the fall term.

Shortly afterward, the still-segregated school began a remarkable run in athletic competition—all of it in the Prairie View Interscholastic League (PVIL). Called the Texas Interscholastic League of Colored Schools when it was founded in 1920, the organization in 1923 came under the authority of Prairie View A&M College and became the PVIL. Dunbar was a 3A school, which represented the largest schools in the PVIL. It won its first state basketball championship in 1953 by beating Odessa Blackshear, 67–53, in the title game.

The 1956–57 school year was an exceptional one for Dunbar High. It won the state basketball title, defeating Baytown Carver, 98–79, and, according to Katie Parks, the state track title later in the spring.

Because Dunbar was experiencing an increase in student enrollment, Lubbock Independent School District officials in 1959 completed a new high school building in the Manhattan Heights Addition at East Twenty-Eighth Street and Teak Avenue. They also transferred the Dunbar name to the modern structure. The former Dunbar building at East Twenty-Sixth and Date Avenue became Iles Elementary School.

In the early 1960s, the Panthers, as the team's nickname and mascot were called, claimed several additional state athletic championships. In 1960, its basketball team beat Houston Elmore, 74–71, for the state 3A title.

Afterward, Dunbar dropped to division 2A. But, as a 2A school in 1962, its basketball team won the state championship by beating Galena Park Fidelity Manor, 63–52, in the final game, and in the spring, its track team, according to Parks, secured the state track title. During the next term, the fall of 1962, Dunbar's football team, wearing used uniforms handed down from Lubbock High School, lost to Wharton Trainer, 40–6, in the championship game. But in the spring of 1963, the Panthers won, according to Parks, its second straight state 2A track title.

Such wins kept coming. In the fall of 1963, after having lost in the title game the previous autumn, Dunbar secured the state football championship by defeating Conroe Washington, 19–14, in the title game. A year and a half later, in 1965, its basketball team won its fifth state title by defeating Cartage Turner, 82–66, in the final game. Finally, according to Parks, during the 1967–68 school year, Dunbar won its fourth state track championship.

About that time, desegregation of schools in Lubbock had begun, and in 1970, Dunbar High School was integrated. By then, the PVIL had disbanded and its schools had joined the University Interscholastic League.

In 1978, Dunbar became Dunbar-Struggs Junior and Senior High School. It graduated its last class in 1993. Today, the building houses the Dunbar

The former Dunbar High School is now Dunbar College Preparatory Academy. *Courtesy June Steele.*

College Preparatory Academy. During most of the championship seasons, Prof Struggs was principal at Dunbar. George Scott was head football coach from 1953 to 1964 during the championship runs. For many years, Damon "Professor" Hill Sr. coached football, basketball and track, but Ernest P. Mallory was coach of most of the championship basketball teams.

One of Dunbar's outstanding athletes was O.D. Gary, a 1955 graduate. Named to the all-state team, he helped lead Dunbar to its first basketball championship in 1953. Curtis Gipson was captain of the 1953 team, and later he was a coach at Dunbar. William Malone was the Panthers' star player on the 1960 title team.

Clearly, Lubbock's Dunbar High School compiled a remarkable athletic record. Over a period of fifteen years, from 1953 to 1968, its students and coaches recorded eleven state athletic championships in the all-black Prairie View Interscholastic League.

42

Early and Late Arrivers on the Plains

German Catholics and Mennonites

David J. Murrah

The vast prairies and isolated farms of the Llano Estacado have long been attractive to groups of religious-based enclaves, such as German-speaking Catholics and Mennonites.

At Stanton, Catholics planted a German colony beginning in 1881 along with a Carmelite monastery. From there, Catholic ministries began in Big Spring, where a church was built in 1888.

After 1900, German Catholic farmers, also encouraged by land promoters, began migrating to the region from the Midwest. At Nazareth, in Castro County, Mass was celebrated by new arrivals in 1903, and the new community grew rapidly. Soon, other immigration led to strong German enclaves and Catholic work at Umbarger, Happy, Olton, Pep, Slaton, Littlefield and Vega.

Although not as numerous as Catholics, Mennonites now number more than two million worldwide and nearly seven hundred thousand in North America. They began as followers of Menno Simons in 1500s Netherlands, who was a part of the Anabaptist movement, which advocated a believer's baptism. Often persecuted, Mennonites generally sought to find a place where they could live in peace rather than fight.

In 1906, Mennonites began immigrating to West Texas when a group from the Midwest purchased land in eastern Hale County near Plainview under the leadership of Mennonite minister Peter B. Snyder. There, they built a schoolhouse, which also served as their church, and by 1909 had a congregation of nearly fifty. The community survived the disastrous drought of 1917–18 but could not sustain through the poor years in the 1920s. In 1925, the church was disbanded as most of the community returned to the Midwest or joined other congregations.

Meanwhile, two other groups of Mennonites purchased land in 1914 near Littlefield in Lamb County, and within two years, the colony had grown to 160. However, the severe drought that began in 1917 on the plains, and the threat of conscription into the U.S. Army, soon decimated the new Mennonite colony. Some remained in Littlefield until the 1940s, even though their church had been sold and moved.

Other Mennonite groups were more successful in the upper Texas Panhandle. In 1943, a group established the Perryton Mennonite Church, and still another group settled the Bethel Mennonite Church at Waka, southwest of Perryton. Later, in 1962, the two congregations merged, and the Perryton church continues to this day. In 1975, Holderman Mennonites moved to Texline and reestablished an earlier colony that had failed in the early 1940s. It is now a thriving community of more than 160 members.

In 1977, two groups of Mennonites purchased land in Gaines and Andrews counties near Seminole and began relocating families from Mexico and Canada. It is now the largest ethnic colony ever established on the Llano Estacado. Both groups came from Old Colony Mennonites who had moved from Canada to Chihuahua, Mexico, in the 1920s. While in Mexico, the colony had outgrown its available land and was attracted to the Llano Estacado for the same reasons as its earlier counterparts: available land and the opportunity to retain their distinctive heritage.

About 250 families, however, were denied entry to the United States, and 43 families were ordered by the immigration and naturalization service to return to Mexico or Canada. Without their presence, the Mennonite leaders could not meet mortgage payments on their land. Their plight gained national attention, and in 1980, the U.S. Congress intervened by passing a bill allowing legalization of approximately six hundred of the colonists. As a result, the colony began to expand and by 2005 had grown to more than five thousand in five churches, making the Seminole colony the largest religious or ethnic enclaves ever established in West Texas.

Due to their multiple migrations in the past century, the Mennonites of West Texas have quite an international heritage. As the Reverend Bill Wiebe, pastor of Gospel Mennonite Church in Seminole, told the *Lubbock Avalanche-Journal* in 2010: "If you're Mennonite, it is likely that your

The Evangelical Mennonite Church in Seminole, Texas, reflects the prosperity the denomination brought to the community. *Courtesy Evangelical Mennonite Church, Seminole, Texas.*

great-grandparents were born in Russia. Your grandparents were born in Canada. You and your parents were born in Mexico. Your children were likely born in Mexico, the U.S. or Canada. Your grandchildren are likely to be born in Canada."

Gaines County has prospered due to the Mennonite influx and has become one of the fastest-growing counties in the area since the 1970s. Other Mennonites have moved to neighboring counties, where they have established productive farms as well. Known as a hardworking, faith-based people, the Mennonites, like the German Catholics before them, have become a great asset for the region.

Part X

SCHOOLS AND SCHOLARS

Since 1923, Texas Tech University has been the dominant component of the Llano Estacado's economic and cultural development. Its creation meant a boom for Lubbock, which eventually became the largest city on the High Plains. Its teachers developed such innovative programs as the Texas Tech Geology Field School held annually in New Mexico.

Texas Tech's growth, spurred by the vision and energy of people like William Curry Holden and his first wife, Olive, ensured that the City of Lubbock would grow and change as well. One important memorial to the Holdens still stands on the Tech campus: the priceless Peter Hurd Mural in the rotunda of Holden Hall.

The chapter concludes with the inspiring story of Mae Murfee, Lubbock's "Wonder Woman," whose life and career has long been an inspiration for Llano Estacado residents.

43

William Curry Holden

David J. Murrah

Curry Holden thought like an entrepreneur. In the spring of 1920, he was twenty-four years old and teaching school in Rotan, Texas. But he knew he needed to find a way to live in Austin so that he could attend the University of Texas. His solution: seek a seat in the Texas legislature.

His campaign against two other young West Texans was nothing like today's mean-spirited politics. Instead, he offered the other two—Charles C. Thompson of Colorado City and R.M. Chitwood of Sweetwater—the opportunity to tour the district with him in his Model T Ford. They all shared meals and gasoline and became good friends and, in time, became permanently emblazoned in Texas Tech history.

Holden lost by a narrow margin to Chitwood. Although his political career was short-lived, in his campaign, Holden strongly advocated for the establishment of a West Texas A&M. He got to see his dream materialize three years later when Texas Tech was created by the legislature as an outgrowth of the West Texas A&M movement.

Holden found another way to get to Austin to pursue a graduate education, and fortunately for West Texas and Texas Tech, he returned to make a major impact on Tech and the region's history and culture.

William Curry Holden was among the very first to research and write West Texas history. He was one of the first archaeologists to identify important historical sites. And, because of his vision, he played a major role in the founding or development of Texas Tech's four major historical and cultural institutions: the Museum of Texas Tech University, the Southwest Collection/Special Collections Library, the National Ranching Heritage Center and the Lubbock Lake Historic Landmark.

William Curry Holden, circa 1944. *Public domain, courtesy Texas State Historical Association, Austin, Texas.*

Born in Limestone County, Texas, in 1896, Curry Holden was two when his family moved to West Texas, where his father struggled in farming near Colorado City and later Rotan. Holden graduated from Rotan High School in 1914, and after obtaining a teaching certificate from Stamford Junior College, he began a teaching career that continued for fifty-two years.

While teaching in public schools, Holden attended summer sessions at West Texas Normal in Canyon and then, in the fall of 1920, entered the University of Texas, where he completed a four-year program in just three years. In 1923, he became head of the history department at the new McMurry College in Abilene. While teaching there, he used his summers to earn two more degrees at the University of Texas, including his PhD in 1928.

Holden's academic success soon attracted the attention of the president of the new Texas Technological College at Lubbock, who hired him to teach both history and anthropology beginning in 1929. "I'd never seen a book on anthropology," Holden later confessed, "so I got a book and stayed two jumps ahead of the students."

Holden soon became an internationally known anthropologist. In 1932, he began field studies of the Yaqui Indians of Sonora, Mexico, and subsequently wrote four books on the subject. He also directed archaeological excavations throughout West Texas and New Mexico. His most significant discovery came at his doorstep, when he identified the great significance of the Lubbock Lake Site as being utilized by every human culture that has occupied North America over more than twelve thousand years.

As a historian, Holden was among the first to write about West Texas. By the time he was thirty-eight, he had written three books, *Alkali Trails*, *Rollie Burns* and *The Spur Ranch*, which still remain definitive works in social and ranching history. In all, Holden wrote twelve books.

Holden also had a brilliant career at Texas Tech, serving as head of the combined departments of history, anthropology and sociology, as well as dean of the Graduate School, and he was instrumental in the establishment of Tech's PhD programs in four fields, including history. For thirty-six years, he served as director of the West Texas Museum.

In that position, he achieved almost the impossible. First, he secured funding in the midst of the Great Depression to build a basement headquarters for the museum; in 1950, he raised funds for its completion, a building that became an imposing structure on the circle at Texas Tech. In all likelihood, it became the first building on the Tech campus to have been erected because of the vision and energy of one person.

Interestingly, by the late 1960s, Texas Tech had named dormitories for the two candidates who had run against Holden in his 1920 campaign for the legislature. Charles Thompson, who became a member of the Texas Tech Board of Directors in 1937 and served as its chair from 1944 to 1957, was honored in 1958 when the school named Thompson Hall for him. Similarly, R.M. Chitwood, who became the school's first business manager in 1924, became the namesake for Chitwood Hall, constructed in 1967.

And so, in 1972, when Texas Tech renovated and enlarged the West Texas Museum building, it was only appropriate that it be named for the third member of that 1920 campaign, William Curry Holden. Today, Holden Hall, with its absolutely priceless Peter Hurd mural, stands as a permanent memorial to the tall, lanky kid from Rotan. He died in 1993. His tombstone in the Lubbock Cemetery records Holden as being simply "a pretty fair country school teacher—with vision."

What a vision it was.

44

The Peter Hurd Mural in Holden Hall

H. Allen Anderson

Almost from the time Texas Technological College opened its doors in the fall of 1925, one of its aims was to better preserve the pioneer past of the Llano Estacado and its Hub City.

Thus, in the spring of 1929, several faculty and administrators, led by Dean of Women Mary Woodward Doak, gathered many townspeople of like interest to form the Plains Museum Society. They also created a museum on the Tech campus. William Curry Holden, who joined the Tech history faculty that summer, took over the museum's curatorial duties. In 1934, it became clear that another, permanent museum facility was needed. But during the Great Depression, funds were short.

Finally, in the Texas centennial year of 1936, the West Texas Museum Association—the name had been changed to maintain a wider regional support—received enough money to construct a basement or ground-floor unit.

Then, in 1950, following World War II, the association obtained funds and state money to complete the upper stories of the building, including a sixteen-sided rotunda.

From the start, the museum association's board of trustees planned to enhance the large rotunda with artwork depicting area history and pioneers. After much deliberation, the trustees decided on a continuous fresco-type mural, completely encircling the rotunda, beginning four feet above the main floor and extending to the mezzanine floor above.

For the artist, they chose the southwestern regionalist Peter Hurd, son-in-law of the late nationally known artist and illustrator N.C. Wyeth. Starting with rough, preliminary charcoal sketches and utilizing techniques dating back to the era of Michelangelo and other Renaissance artists, Hurd commenced work on the fresco in October 1952.

In addition to his wife, portraitist Henriette Wyeth, two protégés, Manuel G. Acosta and John L. Meigs, assisted him. They slaked and cured lime for several months in a pit behind the building to provide smooth mortar for the fresco. Lauro Cavazos, future Texas Tech president, recalled watching Hurd "up [on the scaffold] painting, and it was just a gorgeous addition."

Many curious people dropped by to see the creation of "their mural," and groups of schoolchildren with their teachers came on special field trips to watch the artists at work.

Whenever possible, Hurd had his pioneer subjects sit and pose for him, while others, particularly those who had already passed on, he painted from old photographs and other models selected by their families.

Covering a total of 1,300 square feet of wall space, a near life-size portrait of an area pioneer was painted in each of the sixteen panels, backdropped by an unbroken panorama of daily plains life over a typical twenty-four-hour period during the frontier days around the turn of the twentieth century.

Among the personalities chosen as representative of their time and professions were banker Charles E. Maedgen and university president Clifford B. Jones, both of whom were on the museum board of trustees.

While the entire process took two years, the mural was completed in time for its official dedication on November 18, 1954. Author and historian Paul Horgan, the guest speaker at that dedication ceremony, compared the sixteen figures to the "saints in the Gothic paintings of Europe" and stated that the "media that sustain our human life—air, moisture, light—are imitated upon these walls in magic essence." A thirty-minute color documentary film, *Peter Hurd Paints a Fresco*, was distributed and shown at many museum conferences throughout the nation.

For over fifteen years, the West Texas Museum, with its mural, was the most visited building on the Tech campus. But by the end of the 1960s, a shortage of adequate space for display of its ever-expanding collections of art and artifacts, plus the need for a larger staff, prompted the building of

Artist Peter Hurd placed himself *(left)* and regional scholars in this scene in his famous mural. The gathering around the campfire includes *(left to right)* J. Evetts Haley, William Curry Holden, Tom Lea and John A. Lomax. *Courtesy H. Allen Anderson.*

the present Museum of Texas Tech facility, with its Moody Planetarium, on Lubbock's Fourth Street.

Peter Rogers, Peter Hurd's son-in-law and a muralist in his own right, created a peaceful, pastoral scene emphasizing the importance of water to life on the semi-arid plains. The work was created on the wall above the gift shop near the front entrance, using only black ink, a far different type of media from the Hurd mural.

The former West Texas Museum building was remodeled and transformed into Holden Hall, which now houses the offices of the College of Arts and Sciences and the College of Visual and Performing Arts. Additions for classrooms and office space, erected in the 1970s, house the departments of history, economics and political science.

Students who rush through the rotunda on their way to and from classes often hardly notice the dimly lit showpiece. Yet there are those who do pause and reflect on this visual reminder of the West Texas region's founders and pioneer past.

To this day, the Peter Hurd mural remains as a progenitor to the university's public art and continues to deserve recognition as a prime example of the fresco genre and a true art treasure.

45

Olive Price Holden

Meredith McClain

At the age of nineteen, Ira Olive Price (1902–1937) studied anthropology at the University of Texas in Austin, where, in 1922, she wrote a forty-three-page paper titled "Pueblo Architecture," complete with bibliography and four pages of beautifully executed, hand-drawn illustrations of adobe details. This early passion fueled her entire life.

In 1926, just after Olive married a young historian named William Curry Holden, the couple took a "camping honeymoon" to New Mexico, where Olive introduced her husband to the Pueblos, about which he knew nothing. The trip included a visit to Taos, because Olive knew about the artist colony there and wanted to meet the artists personally, which they did.

In 1929, the Holdens moved with their baby daughter, Jane, from Abilene to Lubbock, where Curry became the chair of the Texas Tech history department and Olive served as reference librarian and instructor of orientation and library research. She also assisted Curry in the development of Tech's anthropology program.

About this time, Olive received $5,000 from her grandmother's estate. With the money, Olive and Curry purchased two lots on Twentieth Street. There, Olive worked with a young architectural student to design a Pueblo Revival style adobe home featuring elements illustrated in her 1922 UT-Austin seminar paper. Hispanic workers made the "'dobes" and built the home, into which Olive and Curry moved in August 1931.

Olive Price Holden and her husband, W. Curry Holden, sit in front of their fireplace in the new home she designed and Curry built in Lubbock in 1934. *Photo from Joe Lewis, "Accidental Collections," http://www.velvethighway.com/joomla/index.php?option=com_content&task=view&id=201&Itemid=114.*

That same year, Olive wrote an article, "Small-town Culture Clubs." In it, she reviewed the history and principles of early founders of such clubs but then critiqued negatively the pretentions of some women in small towns who more recently had joined the clubs mainly to get their names in the local paper and perhaps to avoid housework. Olive concluded, "Our solemn, earnest club pioneers have propagated a queer breed, quite unrecognizable to the venerable Founders. But there are today women of the stature these Founders dreamed of—great lawyers, physicians, educators, artists, homemakers, but none of them belong to a small-town culture club."

Such brutal honesty about lofty ideals motivated Olive at Texas Tech in 1932 to found the Koshari girls' social club, which "sought high scholastic standards, a democratic spirit toward college associates, and encouraged participation in campus activities."

Olive Price Holden, from a portrait. *Courtesy Meredith McClain.*

Olive chose carefully the Hopi word *Koshari*, meaning "delight maker," a word with an ancient, historical, Indian origin. Each spring for years, the Tech Kosharis made an annual Easter trip to Santa Fe, climaxed by an initiation at Arrowhead Kiva.

In the early 1950s, when nationalization of the Tech social clubs became inevitable, the Kosharis became Pi Beta Phi ladies but retained Olive Holden's original Indian themes. In 1984, over one hundred former Kosharis returned to Tech to celebrate their club's fifty-second anniversary.

In 1936, Olive organized and executed a tour to Europe for Curry, his brother Tom and four women friends and then planned two more for the summer of 1937, trips that would include their daughter, Jane, who later became a professor of anthropology.

Olive then set up "Holden Tours" and printed stationery. She also designed a Pueblo-style adobe home for her faculty friend, Dr. Wilbur I. Robinson, which was built on Twenty-Fourth Street south of the Tech campus. Completed in August 1937, it later became known after the 1951 sighting of UFOs there as the "Lubbock Lights House."

A sudden illness befell Olive in April 1937, and after six painful weeks, she passed away. Devastated, Curry Holden wrote:

> *We had the funeral service at home. I think that is where she would have had it, for she loved our house and it was her temple.... There has never been anything that has shocked the college, the town and the surrounding country as much.... There is something marvelous how her personality had influenced the community. She was frail and fragile herself, but she was a tower of strength to hundreds of others who loved her and who felt themselves buoyed up by her spirit....*
>
> *I am going up to Taos to see John Young-Hunter, who was very fond of her, to see if he thinks he can do a portrait of her from such photographs we can get together. The trouble there is, that the thing which made her beautiful was something that was elusive and fleeting—something that no camera could ever catch.... There is nobody else in the world like her, and no one else will ever take her place.*

Led by Pi Beta Phi, a memorial endowment fund in her name was established at Texas Tech. In 1962, during a meeting of the Southwest Collection Trustees and members of Pi Beta Phi, the trustees and the sorority, with Dr. W.C. Holden concurring, agreed to the use of the

Olive Holden Memorial Endowment to buy books for the Southwest Collection.

Holden pointed out that the original endowment "created the idea of the Southwest Collection," now an internationally recognized research center of distinction.

46

Texas Tech's Geology Field School on Nogal Mesa

Paul H. Carlson

Between 1927 and 1941, the geology department at Texas Technological College conducted summer geological field schools in New Mexico.

Leroy Thompson Patton (1880–1956), professor and head of the department from 1925 to 1948, directed the school until 1940, when, he said, he had become "burned out." In that fifteen-year period, he skipped New Mexico during some sessions in order to take students elsewhere, such as Pagosa Springs, Colorado. But for the most part he brought separate groups of students each summer session to Nogal Mesa, southwest of Capitan. In the first years of the field school, Patton and the students traveled in an army-surplus vehicle to New Mexico. It looked like an old bus. Then, in 1930, the college, led by its first president, Paul Whitfield Horn, bought a bus for Patton's use.

In 1927, Patton took eight students to New Mexico. They left Lubbock on June 7 and returned on July 14, the school year's first six-week summer session. They studied rock formations, making notes about their findings, and the students listened to lectures from "Prof" Patton.

The 1927 trip was largely a traveling class. The group of nine rode to Carlsbad, New Mexico, then to Roswell and into Ruidoso. They camped out each night, swam in lakes and rivers where they could and learned about rock formations and what lessons about oil and water the materials might provide. Patton and the students went to Cloudcroft, Alamogordo and

Professor Patton (*right*) with several of his students getting ready to board the old army bus before heading to Nogal Mesa in New Mexico for the summer field school, circa 1930. *Courtesy Southwest Collection, Texas Tech University.*

White Sands, Las Cruces and the Rio Grande. They climbed to the top of Sierra Blanca, where "Prof" at 12,003 feet above sea level gave his students a lecture on the canyons and rock formations below them.

They rode to Capitan and in doing so passed by Nogal Mesa. They also traveled to Carrizozo on U.S. Highway 380 and visited the isolated—and abandoned—pueblos beyond there, where for hundreds of years Indian people had farmed in the desert environment. After returning to Ruidoso, they headed home, passing through Roswell, where they camped on grounds of the thirty-six-year-old New Mexico Military Institute. East of Roswell, they visited Bottomless Lakes, their last stop on the geology trip.

In subsequent years, Patton took students to Central Texas, Pennsylvania and Colorado, but nearly each year during at least one summer session he was in the Ruidoso area. Most often, the Tech students studied at Nogal Mesa. Located between Ruidoso on the southeast, Carrizozo on the northwest and Capitan on the northeast, Nogal Mesa is a flat tabletop some 7,250 to 7,600 feet in elevation. "Traveling east from Carrizozo," writes Gary Cozzens, "one can see the Mesa sitting between Tucson Peak on the left and Nogal Peak on the right." Much "of the area is forest," Cozzens suggests, and "in fact, the Lincoln National Forrest and Smokey Bear Range District occupy a large portion of this land."

The village of Nogal, or what is left of it, on State Highway 37 sits at the western base of the Mesa. Patton often purchased supplies at a store in the tiny town.

In the early years, Patton, who "wore safari-looking clothes, high-laced boots and a desert hat," and the students camped at Nogal Lake. Sometimes, they camped on "Tech Hill," located on a ridge above the now empty Nogal Mesa Ranger Station. They slept in tents at first, but Dick Cox, a member of one of the pioneering families on Nogal Mesa, said, "Tech got an old army barracks and moved it to the top" of the hill. He noted that the students "would stay there, but there was no water supply, so they would…come to our house at Nogal Lake to fill their water container with a garden hose."

In the evenings, while the boys filled their water container, a large tank on wheels pulled behind the bus/truck, and Patton lectured from the truck. "Every evening about five o'clock," Cox also said, the students "went to where a spring came out of the bluff—it was actually a leak" in Nogal Lake. "There was a six-inch pipe that would come out of the bluff and [its water would] hit a rock," he said. "The professor would make the boys take a shower at this site in ice-cold water."

Cox remembered that Patton "would really work the boys. He would have them up early. He had an old army truck with a speaker. He would lecture to the boys while he drove." Patton's students studied rock formations, stream meanderings, canyons and rocky outcroppings. If Cozzens and Cox are correct, they studied outcroppings to see how water ran through the mountains.

Patton directed the field school for the last time in 1939. Two years later, the summer of 1941, was the last time students went up to Tech Hill. "That December," writes Cozzens, "Pearl Harbor was bombed, and they never came back."

47

Mae Murfee

Monte L. Monroe

In 2010, citizens passed a Lubbock Independent School District bond package addressing the needs of twenty-first-century students, but new construction of a school also brought about the loss of an important memorial.

Asbestos problems led to Mae Murfee Elementary School being razed. The student bodies of Murfee and Haynes Elementary Schools were consolidated into a new, larger state-of-the-art institution named Jayne Ann Miller Elementary School. It was determined that the new facility deserved a fresh name. Hence, Miller Elementary School replaced the former Murfee school.

With those changes, the public record of Mae Murfee's historic service to the community vanished, and the memorabilia associated with the demolished school was returned to the family, including a state historical marker about her life.

Eva Mae Murfee was born in Nesbitt, Haskell County, Texas, the daughter of James Edward "J.E." and Sarah Emily Griffin Murfee. Her father was an early Lubbock County pioneer and among its first prominent land developers. Though raised on the last Texas frontier, Mae Murfee, as she was commonly known, rejoiced in learning, and she gained an education that benefited generations of students in Lubbock County and the state of Texas.

Murfee was ahead of her time. In 1905, she taught in the Block 20 School at the original community of Slide and also served as principal

Mae Murphee, circa 1910. *Courtesy Murphee family and the Southwest Collection, Texas Tech University.*

there. In 1909, she furthered her education at Texas Woman's College, from which she was graduated. She carried out additional graduate work through the University of California and Georgetown University in Washington, D.C. In 1914, she became the first woman principal of Lubbock Junior High.

Recognizing a critical educational need in the community, Murfee in 1916 gifted her own books to create Lubbock High's first school library.

For many years, Murfee headed the history and government departments at Lubbock High School, garnering the first state accreditation for those courses in the district. She was a trailblazer in the use of visual aids in the classroom, purchasing equipment with personal funds to benefit her students. Murfee even forged the first connection between the Lubbock School District and the Interscholastic League.

Miss Murfee's contributions to education in Lubbock continued. In the early 1920s, when it was uncommon for women to be involved in such matters, she was a strong advocate for and became the only woman on the steering committee that worked to locate Texas Technological College in Lubbock. In fact, she personally funded a two-story boardinghouse as her personal contribution to the cause. It housed students for over fifty years.

In 1928, she ran for and became the Lubbock County school superintendent of education, holding the key position until 1936. In this work, she led efforts to standardize educational practices across the county. She introduced home economics, a health nurse and libraries into Lubbock County schools.

Murfee also served as the area's six-county district supervisor for the Texas Department of Education, becoming well known throughout the state as an educational advocate, especially as an agitator for free textbooks in Texas schools. Also, Murfee was extensively involved in civic service activities. She served on local, district and state boards and as an officer or president of organizations, including the Texas Federation of Women's Clubs, the League of Women Voters, the Crippled Children's Society, the Boy Scouts of America and the state Centennial Committee.

She was instrumental in establishing the Allen Brothers VFW Post 148 and the Ladies Auxiliary. She had been closely involved in civic activities during World War I and World War II, being awarded citations by the U.S. president, the War Department and the State Commission for War Service.

Murfee worked with the first chamber of commerce to bring water and lights to Lubbock, was on the state commission to prevent tuberculosis, was supervisor for the state organization on child welfare and actively campaigned for pure food laws. She helped organize Delta Kappa Gama Sorority; was the county and district chair of the Democratic Party, attending a national convention; and was state chair of the Texas Conservation of Natural Resources Committee. She was a member and officer at the state, district and local level of numerous historical and cultural organizations, and she faithfully served the First Methodist Church of Lubbock for over fifty years, having a window placed in her honor.

Murfee even provided monetary support for young students like David Hester to travel oversees to broaden their horizons. She believed that "every boy and girl may be saved to useful citizenship if the right person is there at the right time—the parent or the teacher." A century before the accomplishments of women in modern society were proclaimed as commonplace, Mae Murfee was among the vanguard of her gender, giving of her time, resources and talents to the betterment of her community. She garnered numerous honors.

The many accomplishments and varied talents of this early South Plains "Wonder Woman" should be recognized in conspicuous fashion. They will inspire future generations of young women and, indeed, of all Lubbock citizens.

Selected Bibliography

Abbe, Donald, Paul H. Carlson and David J. Murrah. *Lubbock and the South Plains: An Illustrated History*. 2nd ed. Tarzana, CA: Preferred Marketing, 1995.

Blodgett, Jan. *Land of Bright Promise: Advertising the Texas Panhandle and South Plains, 1870–1917*. Austin: University of Texas Press, 1988.

Carlson, Paul H. *Amarillo: The Story of a Western Town*. Lubbock: Texas Tech University Press, 2006.

———. *The Buffalo Soldier Tragedy of 1877*. College Station: Texas A&M University Press, 2003.

———. *Deep Time and the Texas High Plains: History & Geology*. Lubbock: Texas Tech University Press, 2005.

———. *Empire Builder in the Texas Panhandle: William Henry Bush*. College Station: Texas Tech University Press, 1996.

Carlson, Paul H., and David J. Murrah, eds. *Hidden History of the Llano Estacado*. Charleston, South Carolina: The History Press, 2017.

Fleming, Elvis E., and David J. Murrah. *Texas' Last Frontier: A New History of Cochran County*. Morton, TX: Cochran County Historical Commission, 2001.

Glasrud, Bruce, and Paul H. Carlson with Tai D. Kreidler, eds. *Slavery to Integration: Black Americans in West Texas*. Abilene: State House Press, 2007.

Gracy, David B. II. *A Man Absolutely Sure of Himself: Texan George Washington Littlefield.* Norman: University of Oklahoma Press, 2019.

———. *Littlefield Lands: Colonization on the Texas Plains, 1912–1920*. Austin: University of Texas Press, 1968.

Haley, J. Evetts. *Charles Goodnight: Cowman and Plainsman*. Boston: Houghton Mifflin Company, 1936.

———. *The XIT Ranch of Texas and the Early Days of the Llano Estacado*. Garden City, NY: Doubleday, 1976.

Hamalainnen, Pekka. *The Comanche Empire*. New Haven, CT: Yale University Press, 2008.

Holiday, Vance T. *Paleoindian Geoarchaeology of the Southern High Plains*. Foreword by Thomas R. Hester. Austin: University of Texas Press, 1997.

Hunt, George M. *Early Days Upon the Plains of Texas*. Lubbock: Avalanche Publishing Company, 1919.

Kenner, Charles L. *The Comanchero Frontier: A History of New Mexican-Plains Indian Relations*. Norman: University of Oklahoma Press, 1994.

Morris, John Miller. *El Llano Estacado: Exploration and Imagination on the High Plains of Texas and New Mexico, 1536–1860*. Austin: Texas State Historical Association, 1997.

Murrah, David J. *"And Are We Yet Alive?" A History of the Northwest Texas Conference of the United Methodist Church*. Foreword by Bishop D. Max Whitfield. Buffalo Gap, TX: State House Press, 2009.

———. *C.C. Slaughter: Rancher, Banker, Baptist*. Austin: University of Texas Press, 1981.

———. *Oil, Taxes, and Cats: A History of the Devitt Family and the Mallet Ranch*. Lubbock: Texas Tech University Press, 1994.

Rathjen, Fred. *The Texas Panhandle Frontier*. Rev. ed. Introduction by Elmer Kelton. Lubbock: Texas Tech University Press, 1998.

Tijerina, Andres A. *A History of Mexican Americans in Lubbock County, Texas*. Lubbock: Texas Tech University Press, 1979.

Wallace, Ernest. *Ranald S. Mackenzie on the Texas Frontier*. Lubbock: West Texas Museum Association, 1964.

Worster, Donald. *The Dust Bowl: The Southern Plains in the 1930s*. New York: Oxford University Press, 1979.

Index

C

D

E

H

I

J

T

U

V

W

X

Y

About the Contributors

Donald Abbe, PhD, is former curator of history at the Silent Wings Museum in Lubbock and historian of the Llano Estacado region.

Sally Still Abbe, MA, is a Lubbock historian and serves as director of data services for the City of Lubbock.

H. Allen Anderson, PhD, is a senior archival associate and historian for the Southwest Collection/Special Collections Library at Texas Tech.

Jack Becker, MLS, MA, is a librarian at Texas Tech University and the author of three books relating to West Texas.

Ashley Pettiet Branch, MA, is curator of the King County Historical Museum and teaches social studies at Guthrie High School.

Ray Cragar lives in Lubbock and has long been interested in natural history.

Duane Hale, PhD, is professor of history at Cisco College in Cisco, Texas.

Chuck Lanehart, JD, is a criminal defense attorney and legal historian in Lubbock, Texas.

Meredith McClain, PhD, retired from Texas Tech University in 2013 as associate professor emeritus of foreign languages.

Monte Monroe, PhD, is an archivist for the Southwest Collection/Special Collections Library at Texas Tech University and currently serves as the Texas State Historian.

Dolores Mosser of Lubbock is a children book's author and historian of the western Llano Estacado.

Dan'l Richardson lives in Lubbock and is a student of the history of the Llano Estacado.

Sammie Simpson of Maple, Texas, is chief historian of Bailey County, Texas.

June Steele, MA, teaches history and social studies at Monterey High School in Lubbock.

Christena Stephens, MS, is a writer, fine-art photographer, nonprofit geek and outdoor enthusiast living in Sundown, Texas.

About the Editors

David J. Murrah, PhD, is a museum and historical consultant. He served for twenty-five years as archivist and director of the Southwest Collection at Texas Tech University before entering the museum exhibit/design field with Southwest Museum Services of Houston. He has written or edited eight books and numerous articles on Texas history and is a fellow of both the Texas State Historical Association and the West Texas Historical Association. A native of the High Plains (Gruver, Texas), he and his wife, Ann, now live on the Texas coast at Rockport.

Paul H. Carlson, PhD, is a member of the Texas Institute of Letters and the Philosophical Society of Texas. As emeritus professor of history at Texas Tech University, he is the author of numerous books and articles and editor of others. A fellow of both the Texas State Historical Association and the West Texas Historical Association, he is also the recipient of several university teaching awards. For more than thirty-five years, he and his wife, Ellen, have lived in historic Ransom Canyon at the very edge of the Llano Estacado.